Walking in community with Leighann, we know firsthand that she has lived the things she teaches. What you are reading is a work that has been tested. Leighann is a living testimony that radical pursuit of a relationship with Jesus through prayer will result in a radically changed life. Jump in . . . draw close . . . and be changed . . . by a faithful life of prayer.

—TRAVIS COTTRELL
WORSHIP LEADER, BETH MOORE CONFERENCES/RECORDING ARTIST

The quoted ideas expressed in this book (but not Scripture verses) are not, in all cases, exact quotations, as some have been edited for clarity and brevity. In all cases, the author has attempted to maintain the speaker's original intent. In some cases, quoted material for this book was obtained from secondary sources, primarily print media. While every effort was made to ensure the accuracy of these sources, the accuracy cannot be guaranteed. For additions, deletions, corrections, or clarifications in future editions of this text, please write Freeman-Smith.

Unless otherwise noted all Scripture quotations are taken from:

The Holy Bible, New International Version (NIV) Copyright © 1973, 1978, 1984, by International Bible Society. Used by permission of Zondervan Publishing House. All rights reserved.

Scripture quotations are taken from:

The Holy Bible, King James Version (KJV)

The Holy Bible, New King James Version (NKJV) Copyright © 1982 by Thomas Nelson, Inc. Used by permission.

The New American Standard Bible®, (NASB) Copyright © 1960, 1962, 1963, 1968, 1971, 1972, 1973, 1975, 1977, 1995 by The Lockman Foundation. Used by permission.

The Holman Christian Standard Bible™ (HCSB) Copyright © 1999, 2000, 2001 by Holman Bible Publishers. Used by permission.

Cover Design by Kim Russell / Wahoo Designs
Page Layout by Bart Dawson

ISBN 978-1-60587-371-8
ISBN 978-1-60587-409-8 (Special Edition)

1 2 3 4 5—SBI—16 15 14 13 12

Printed in the United States of America

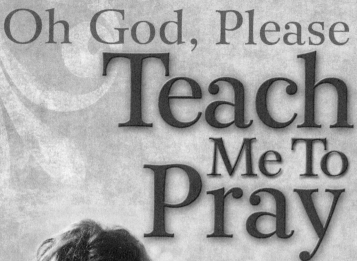

Oh God, Please Teach Me To Pray

LEIGHANN MCCOY

Table of Contents

Introduction

This is the confidence we have in approaching God: that if we ask anything according to his will, he hears us. And if we know that he hears us—whatever we ask—we know that we have what we asked of him.

— 1 JOHN 5:14–15

There you have it. In 1 John the Bible teaches that when you pray you can expect God to do great things in and through your life. In fact, in John 15:5 Jesus says that you can do nothing apart from Him, so why don't you spend more time with Him?

If you're like me, you've been baffled by prayer since you recited the sing song children's blessing at mealtimes: "God is great, God is good. Let us thank Him for our food . . . ." I can still remember bowing my head, folding my hands, and meaning every word that came out of my mouth. But as I grew up, I discovered needs that went far deeper than those that were satisfied by a peanut butter sandwich, and that little blessing I memorized as a child didn't suffice.

The *Oh God, Please* series will help you discover the powerful privilege of prayer. In the pages of these books, you will learn that prayer is far more than singsong blessings. As you read you will confront the voices that barge their way into your mind and war against you when you pray. You will discover how to take your thoughts captive to the lordship of Christ (2 Corinthians 10:5) and channel your heart cries into canals that draw you closer and closer to the heart of God and the mind of Christ.

When you read these books, you will learn that prayer is a relationship and not a list, not a meeting or a method. Many believers today fail to pray because they are deceived into thinking prayer doesn't work, but as you read, you will discover that prayer is often the only thing that does work!

Each book in the *Oh God, Please* series will remind you that the all-powerful, all-loving God longs to demonstrate His power and love in and through your life as you partner with Him in His kingdom work. You partner with God when you pray. God is more interested in teaching you to pray than you are in learning. He is also more interested in answering your prayers than you are in praying them.

Welcome to *Oh God, Please Teach Me to Pray.* The book you're holding in your hands will help you capture and subdue the voice of doubt that keeps you from learning to pray. By reading you will learn that prayer is a two-way conversation and that learning to hear God's voice is just as critical to success in prayer as Him hearing yours. You will learn what prayer is and what prayer is not.

This book is for you if you feel like your attempt to talk to God bounces off the ceiling and conks you on the head. This book is for you if you've exhausted every angle, every acrostic, every verse, and still . . . God seems distant. This book is for you if you want to know how to pray.

PART 1

Prayer Is . . . Intimacy

Prayer is not overcoming God's reluctance
but laying hold of His willingness.

—

MARTIN LUTHER

CHAPTER 1

Intimacy with God

"My prayer is not for them alone. I pray also for those who will believe in me through their message, that all of them may be one, Father, just as you are in me and I am in you. May they also be in us so that the world may believe that you have sent me."

— JOHN 17:20-21

Intimacy with God. Is that even possible? Who can begin to comprehend the Mastermind of the universe? Who are we to dare to approach the Creator and Sustainer of life with any thought at all of being in a personal relationship with Him?

If God hadn't come to us, we wouldn't have a chance. But I've got good news; God did come to us. He came to you! "The Word became flesh and dwelt among us" (John 1:14). And He is the One who beseeches you to come to Him. "Come to me all you who are weary and burdened and I will give you rest" (Matthew 11:28). God invites you to have intimacy with Him.

What Does Intimacy with God Look Like?

God uses several earthly relationships to describe His love for us. Jesus called God His "Father" and taught us that we are God's sons and daughters. In Isaiah 49:15 God said His love toward us was more precious than the love a mother has for her nursing baby. Several times throughout Scripture God is called our Master, our Good Shepherd, the King of kings, and the Lord of lords.

But in order to describe the intimacy that God longs to have with us, let's look at the marriage relationship. This illustration was given to Paul in the letter he wrote to the Ephesians. I'm not going to reprint the verses here, but you will get more out of this chapter if you will get your Bible and read Ephesians 5:22–33

> Prayer is the avenue by which we attain intimacy with God.

and underline every reference Paul made to Christ and the church. You will find the words in verses 23, 24, 25–27, 29–30, and especially in 32: "This is a profound mystery—*but I am talking about Christ and the church*" (italics added).

Most often we hear these verses from Ephesians taught with the emphasis being on wives submitting to their husbands and husbands loving their wives. And while this is a great place to learn how a godly marriage works, when Paul penned these words his emphasis was on the intimacy Christ has with His church.

I happen to be married. In fact, as I am writing this book I am exactly two weeks away from my twenty-fifth wedding anniversary. Therefore I am thrilled to share with you my living illustration of the mystery of intimacy God longs to share with us.

I met Tom McCoy in October of 1985. We'd just begun our first semester of graduate studies at Southwestern Seminary in Ft. Worth, Texas. I lived with two students I'd recently met. One of my roommates, Georgia, had a class with Tom where she was immediately drawn in by what I call the "McCoy charisma." A few days before Tom and I actually met, she pointed him out to me when we were sitting at a traffic light where Seminary Drive and McCart Avenue intersect. I couldn't tell if he was a "looker" because the car he drove had tinted windows. But on the fateful Sunday night that followed, Tom and his friend Bert came to see Georgia, at 1009 James Avenue, and Tom saw me instead.

A few days later, I came home from work and bumped into Tom and Georgia coming back from a jog. He later confessed that the only reason he'd booked a jogging date with Georgia was in hopes of seeing me. The next day, when I came home from work Tom just happened to be there to borrow the mower from Jackie (my other roommate). It was on this errand, standing on the back porch of our little rental house, when Tom asked me out.

I said yes.

I am not even going into the dynamics of my relationship with Georgia, but I'll just say that she eventually talked to me again and then took credit for our marriage.

Amidst Georgia's frustration with me, Tom and I had our first date. He took me to the Chinese Kitchen. This was not a classy restaurant, but we were poor and I was a bit smitten by his charm and good looks. So what if I had to balance my plastic red tray and plate of chicken chow mien with a free egg roll washed down with water in a Styrofoam cup?

I can't even remember what that food tasted like, but I do remember the Chinese Kitchen conversation. We munched on our fried rice, and I began with my list of "Questions to Ask on the First Date When Your Date Doesn't Talk."

1. Do you have any brothers or sisters?
   "Three brothers, no sisters."
2. What sports did you play growing up?
   "Tennis in college, baseball, football, basketball."
3. When did you start lifeguarding?
   "When I was fifteen."

4. Why did you come to seminary?
   "I think God is calling me to be an evangelist. I like to preach."
5. Why did you choose Southwestern?
   "It's where my best friend came."
6. Tell me about becoming a Christian.
   "My dad's a pastor, and I thought I was saved when I was seven but didn't understand until I was nineteen and in college."

This charming man who'd mesmerized me at my kitchen table on Sunday night was suddenly unable to do more than fill in the blanks on my questionnaire at the Chinese Kitchen. After trying to stoke him into a conversation, I was grateful that he'd planned to take me to the dollar movie theater where our action hero could take over the conversation.

Oh, those first dates! The only thing worse than our first date was the turmoil that rocked and rolled in between his phone calls.

- What if he doesn't call, what if he does?
- What's he thinking?
- Does he like me?
- Do I like him?
- And the most difficult of all: If he does call—and I do want him to—if he does like me and I like him, and he actually asks me out on another date, what should I wear?

Remember the apprehension, the fear, the uncertainty? "Keep a rein on those emotions. You don't want them to be trampled. Be careful; guard your heart!"

Today I am once again surfing the waves of young romantic relationships. My children are 16, 18, and 19. One is married; the other two are still dating. Here are some phrases I hear often: "I'm never taking your advice again!" "I like him SO much, Mommy!" And the next day—"I hate him! Boys are so stupid!" Or "Oh Mama, you are so smart—it worked!" (Maybe that comment was one I made up in the fog that happens just before dawn between sleep and wishful thinking.)

I am so glad I'm out of the dating game. Marriage is tough but dating is brutal!

But, as Tom and I spent more time together, the attraction grew and trust gradually developed. On another Sunday afternoon, he looked into my eyes and made a verbal confession of his love. After that there was a promise, a few gifts, and finally the ring.

The rest is history.

Oh God, Please . . .

If you are reading this book with a group of people, consider sharing your responses to the following statements and questions. If you are reading this book on your own, jot your answers down in your prayer journal.

1. If you are married, reflect on the early days of your dating relationship. Share how you met your spouse and what thoughts and feelings you had during the early days of your acquaintance.

2. Describe the difference between falling in love with another and being committed to love another.

3. How is your relationship with God like your relationship with your spouse? How is it different?

4. If you are single, how is your relationship with God like the relationship you have with a dear friend? How is it different?

Pray: *Lord, I want to know You more. I want to get beyond the "first date" kind of relationship and grow toward intimacy. Thank You for teaching me to pray. Amen*

CHAPTER 2

Intimacy Develops Over Time

"May they be brought to complete unity to let the world know that you sent me and have loved them even as you have loved me."

— JOHN 17:23B

Today Tom is my best friend and my intimate companion. We've made children together; we've grown a church together; we've built a patio, closed in a garage, put up a play set, bought a boat, and tiled a bathroom floor (well, from the patio forward he did those things mostly himself, but I supported him every step of the way). We've even made a mess of things together.

We talk; we go places together; we laugh; we cry. We might even simply touch our fingers to the other's as we walk to the graveside of a thirty-one-year-old man who has just lost his battle with lung cancer, and without exchanging anymore than a gentle touch we've said much.

Not long ago Tom and I spread a blanket in the woods on the side of a mountain in Blowing Rock, North Carolina, and I penned these words. I started talking to him, and he asked, "Are you working on something?" I responded that yes, in fact, I was. He said, "Well, get to working." And even with that we were experiencing intimacy, communication, and all that goes with being *one* with each other.

Be Still and Know

Let's go back to 1985. When Tom and I were together, we hardly ever experienced intimacy. What we had was time—and confusion and awkward silence and all kinds of other things—but it could hardly be called intimacy.

Why was it so difficult to establish that intimacy early on? Because neither one of us was sure how the other person was feeling. We both harbored fears of rejection. And neither of us really knew the other one very well. I didn't have a clue that he withdrew when he was confused or tired. He had no idea that my mind was always running thoughts through it in warp speed. I didn't know that he saw most things black and white while I was seeing everything in living color (and with lots of those colors blended)!

We didn't experience intimacy because we didn't know each other very well. As we became acquainted, we grew to understand each other; we were better able to communicate.

God desires intimacy with you, and prayer is the way you develop this intimacy. When you pray, do you experience intimacy with God? Or, are your prayers like my Chinese Kitchen experience?

> *Uh, it's me here, Lord! Thou hast made a glorious day this day, and I hope Thou hast enjoyed it as much as I hath.*

Why is it we think we have to speak in the King James Version to be heard by God?! Do you talk to God and run out of things to say?

> *Uh-oh, I know, I'll use the alphabet to think of all the reasons I love You today!*
> *A—awesome—You are awesome, yeah.*
> *B—beautiful—all that You do is beautiful . . . .*

And you go along pretty good until you get to *K*.

Krafty.

No, that's a C unless you're talking about salad dressing.

Kool.

C again unless you're talking Kool-Aid . . . . Do you wonder why God doesn't talk to you?

> *Uh, Lord, it's me again. I'm doing good. We've talked like this every day this week, and I feel really good about it. So where did we leave off yesterday? Oh, I remember. Monday's the missionaries. Did that. Tuesdays are for turkeys—all the people I don't like too much. Thank goodness we got through that. And today's Wednesday— so it's time to talk to you about the Weally Wonderful people. Great, Lord, bless my husband. I know he was on the list yesterday, but today he's being weally wonderful. And bless my children; they are so wonderful. Go ahead and bless my friends Kathleen, Jeanie, Joann, Edna, Margaret, Inez, . . .*

Then you pause and look at the clock, wondering how much time until you've reached ten minutes.

> *Hmmm, three more minutes. Hmmm . . .*
>
> *Jackie, . . .*

And you spend the rest of your time in prayer considering whether you have a friend for every letter of the alphabet. Ten minutes are up, and you say,

> *In Jesus' name, amen. Check! Prayed on Wednesday.*

Do any of these prayer times resemble your own? Perhaps, like me when Tom and I first started dating, you struggle with God's interest in you. What if He doesn't care?

> *Lord, who am I that You want to listen to me? I yelled at my children yesterday, ate chocolate when I swore I wouldn't do that anymore, turned the TV on and couldn't turn it off—Oprah was doing a special on support bras!*

Or

> *Lord, we're all out of money, and it's only the fifth day of the month. We don't get paid for three more weeks, and we blew it—it's all our fault; I know we just have to own this. You've got much better things to concern Yourself with, like supporting the missionaries who live in Zambia and give away all their extra bread to feed poor orphans.*

What if God won't answer? What if He's not there?

In Romans 5:6–8 Paul reminds us that God has already made the first declaration of His love: "You see, at just the right time, when we were still powerless, Christ died for the ungodly. Very rarely will anyone die for a righteous man, though for a good man someone might possibly dare to die. But God demonstrates his own love for us in this: While we were still sinners, Christ died for us."

> No matter where you are in your prayer life, God desires intimacy with you.

Therefore you can approach the adventure of intimacy with God without fear of rejection. Unlike dating, when you enter into a personal relationship with God, you enter the relationship already knowing how He feels about you.

God loves you and desires intimacy with you.

Oh God, Please . . .

If you are reading this book with a group of people, consider sharing your responses to the following questions. If you are reading this book on your own, jot your answers down in your prayer journal.

1. Think about the person you consider your most intimate companion. How did your first impressions change as you got to know him/her better?

2. Prayer involves getting to know God better. How can you get to know God better this week?

3. Read Ephesians 5:22–33 and Romans 5:6–8. How do these passages of Scripture impact your prayer life?

Pray: *Lord, thank You for declaring Your love for me. It's a bit overwhelming to consider that You choose to love me, but I am grateful. I want to know You more. I want to learn what it means to genuinely understand You. Please teach me to pray. Amen*

CHAPTER 3

Jesus Prayed for Oneness

"I have given them the glory that you gave me, that they may be one as we are one: I in them and you in me . . . ."

— JOHN 17:22–23A

God loves you and desires intimacy with you. Let these words soak in your mind. Say them aloud. "God loves me and desires intimacy with me."

This truth is woven throughout Scripture, from the creation of Adam and Eve in Genesis to the "Amen" at the end of Revelation. But God's desire for intimacy with us is best described in John 17, where we get to eavesdrop on Jesus' prayer life.

Most of the prayers that Jesus prayed are not recorded in the Gospels because Jesus often went off by Himself to communicate with His Father. But in one particularly intimate moment, Jesus' disciples were invited to listen as He poured His heart out to God.

John 17, more than any other chapter of the Bible, describes the deep desire that God has for an intimate, personal relationship with us. And because prayer is the avenue for that intimacy to develop, I want to invite you to walk with me through a verse-by-verse discussion. Open your Bible to John 17 as you read this chapter.

Background

If you go back a few chapters to John 13, you will discover where Jesus was when He spoke these words. He and His disciples were lounging together after the evening meal (which happened to be the last time they would observe the Passover together). Jesus made Peter (and most likely the other disciples) uncomfortable by washing their feet, and He'd dismissed His traitor, Judas Iscariot.

> *"I have told you these things, so that in me you may have peace. In this world you will have trouble. But take heart! I have overcome the world."*
>
> —JOHN 16:33

Once Judas was gone, Jesus began to share His heart with His disciples. He wanted to prepare them for His approaching death. They'd walked with him for three years and understood many things, but their faith was about to be shaken to the core. Jesus knew that everything He'd told them about the kingdom of God and the victory that was theirs as new citizens of this kingdom was about to be challenged.

So He spoke. He uttered some of the greatest words in all of Scripture.

> *"Do not let your hearts be troubled. Trust in God; trust also in me."*
>
> —JOHN 14:1

> *"I am the way and the truth and the life. No one comes to the Father except through me."*
>
> —JOHN 14:6

"I tell you the truth, anyone who has faith in me will do what I have been doing. He will do even greater things than these."

—JOHN 14:12

"And I will do whatever you ask in my name, so that the Son may bring glory to the Father. You may ask me for anything in my name, and I will do it."

—JOHN 14:13–14

"If you love me, you will obey what I command."

—JOHN 14:15

"Whoever has my commands and obeys them, he is the one who loves me. He who loves me will be loved by my Father, and I too will love him and show myself to him."

—JOHN 14:21

Then there is the entire chapter of John 15, where Jesus taught His disciples the principles of the vine. In John 16 He described the work of the Holy Spirit and promised His coming. Then Jesus gave His disciples (and us) this great promise: "I have told you these things, so that in me you may have peace. In this world you will have trouble. But take heart! I have overcome the world" (John 16:33).

Jesus knew His death was right around the corner, and just as any friend—or even a parent—would do, in John 17 He then began to pray for those who would be left behind. Let's look at this prayer and discover how it demonstrates God's desire for intimacy with us.

A Closer Look at John 17

Jesus Prayed for Himself: John 17:1–5

Jesus' first request was that God bring glory to Himself by glorifying His Son. Jesus stated His purpose in John 17:2 ("that he might give eternal life"), then He gave His Father a report of His own work: "I have brought you glory on earth by completing the work you gave me to do" (v. 4).

What a powerful statement! I hope that if I have the sober privilege of knowing when my last minutes on earth have come I can say what Jesus said, "I have brought You glory on earth by completing the work You gave me to do."

Jesus Celebrated His Work: John 17:6–9

After Jesus prayed for Himself, He expanded on the report to His Father concerning the work He had done while He was here: "I have revealed you to those whom you gave me out of the world."

Notice who Jesus revealed God to: "those whom you gave me" (John 17:6).

If you have your Bible, turn to Luke 6:12–16 and read those verses to discover how Jesus went about choosing the men who would be His disciples. Prior to naming the Twelve, Jesus went out to a mountainside to pray. He spent the entire night praying to God.

Because Jesus talked to God about which men should be His disciples, He did not wonder if He'd made the wrong decision when Peter denied Him. Jesus didn't feel defeated when Judas betrayed Him. Jesus did not wring His hands in despair when James and John argued over the exalted positions in His kingdom's government. Jesus didn't call a screeching halt to the crucifixion proceedings when every one of His followers deserted Him.

Jesus *knew* these were the men God chose to build the foundation of His church because He'd prayed all night for specific direction. Jesus' confidence in the future of His church was never based on the actions and attitudes of His disciples. Jesus' confidence in His church was and is based on the power and activity of the Holy Spirit!

Can you hear Jesus' enthusiasm as He gives His Father this report? It reminds me of the interaction between a father and a son after a great plan comes together beautifully.

When my father turned sixty, my sisters and I planned a huge celebration. It began with a surprise greeting at his gate at the Hartsfield International Airport in Atlanta, Georgia, as he returned from his weekly commute to Chicago. (This was before the security restrictions that went into effect after 9-11.) All of my sisters and our husbands (from NC, TX, FL, and TN), along with our babies in tow, greeted Dad with banners, balloons, and noisemakers. For years after, we relived that moment when my family got together. "Don't you remember the look on his face? What about grandma in her wheelchair? He was surprised, definitely surprised."

> Jesus' confidence in the future of His church was never based on the actions and attitudes of His disciples.

Oh how we enjoyed celebrating our job well done. That which we carefully, lovingly planned we executed together, and together we enjoyed great success.

This is how I think of Jesus' report. "Father, I showed them who You are, just like we planned! They know everything I have comes from You. I told them what You told me to say, and they believed. It worked! We did it!"

Oh God, Please . . .

Either share your answers with your group, or record your thoughts in your prayer journal.

1. Imagine you are standing before God giving a report on the work you did on earth. What might your report include?

2. What part of Jesus' prayer demonstrates the intimacy He shared with His Father?

3. How do your prayers demonstrate intimacy with God?

> **Pray:** *Thank You, Lord, for choosing death on a cross so that I could have more than a distant relationship with You. Thank You for inviting me into a relationship that is real and intimate. I am so grateful for what You've done. I don't want to miss any of the riches You purchased for me through Your death on the cross. I want to grow in my relationship with You. Amen*

CHAPTER 4

Jesus Prayed for Us

He is able to save completely those who come to God through him, because he always lives to intercede for them.

— HEBREWS 7:25

Y̶ou are reading this book right now because Jesus is interceding on your behalf. Look at the time. No matter what your clock says—whether it is 5:14 a.m., 10:43 a.m., 9:27 p.m., 11:20 p.m., or 2:13 a.m.—Jesus is sitting at the right hand of His Father (a place of privilege and authority), and He is praying for you.

Jesus Prayed for His Disciples: John 17:9–19

One of the sweetest sentences in God's Word is "I pray for them" (John 17:9). Jesus, God's Son—the One who knows us best and loves us perfectly—is ever interceding on our behalf. Hebrews 7:25 says, "He is able to save completely those who come to God through him, because he always lives to intercede for them."

As you read Jesus' prayer for His disciples, you can quickly discover His main concern. Read John 17:15: "My prayer is not that you take them out of the world but that you protect them from the evil one."

Do you hear His heart? Jesus is concerned that His disciples remain protected from the schemes and deceptions of the "evil one" now that He will no longer be with them. He seems to be saying, "Now that I've revealed truth to them, they are no longer of this world. The world will hate them. Don't take them out of the world; just protect them from the evil one!"

How does God protect us from the evil one? He tells us how in John 17:17: "Sanctify them by the truth; your word is truth."

Notice first that Jesus did not pray for the physical safety of His disciples. He already knew and had already told them that they would be persecuted for their faith and some of them would suffer a martyr's death because of their loyalty to Him. The church we pledge allegiance to is established on the blood of Jesus and built on the blood of His followers.

Jesus asked God to give His disciples spiritual protection. He knew Satan was cunning and deceiving. Satan continues to be cunning and deceptive today. Satan is intent on breeding doubt and despair into your prayer life.

> Jesus, God's Son—the One who knows us best and loves us perfectly—is ever interceding on our behalf.

During the Kuwait conflict (a prelude in the early 1990s to the war with Iraq that came later and cost Americans much), we discovered that we had a powerful weapon called the "Patriot missile." It was designed to detect, target, and then neutralize enemy missiles. We heard all about the effectiveness of this marvelous weapon when our enemy launched Scud missile attacks against our allies in Israel and us.

The best Patriot missile we have as followers of Christ is God's Word. To render Satan's Scud attacks powerless, immerse yourself in God's Word, which is truth. Memorize Scripture; use the promises of God against the onslaught of Satan.

When Satan challenges God's goodness—when he flaunts the conflict that often exists between your reality and God's promises—cling tightly to God's promises. Don't ever forget that God's Word is truth, and Satan's goal is to deceive you into believing that somehow God is not capable of fulfilling His Word in your life. If Satan convinces you that God cannot be trusted, you will not pray. Or, you will pray without faith. When you pray without faith, you will struggle needlessly with anxiety and fear.

Intercept Satan's Scud attack with the Word of God. One of the most powerful prayers you can pray is Scripture, and one of the best places to find Scripture prayers is in the book of Psalms. Pray the Psalms, and wait expectantly for God to prove true to His Word.

After Jesus prayed for His disciples' protection, He asked God to leave them in the world a bit longer for a specific purpose: "As you sent me into the world, I have sent them into the world" (John 17:18).

Like the original followers of Jesus, we have been given the same assignment that God gave His Son: to make Him known among the nations. When Jesus spoke these words, only one thing was yet to be done, and that one thing is found in verse 19: "For them I sanctify myself, that they too may be truly sanctified." In essence Jesus said, "I am setting myself apart to do what You want me to do so my disciples may also be set apart to do what You want them to do."

The disciples had faith and understanding, but their sin still kept them eternally condemned in the presence of a holy God. So, Jesus paid the penalty for their sin—for our sin—so they—and we—could truly experience a personal, intimate relationship with Him.

Jesus Prayed for Us: John 17:20–23

In John 17:20 Jesus said these precious words: "My prayer is not for them alone. I pray also for those who will believe in me through their message." He had you on His mind when He said those words. Say the following aloud: "My prayer is not for them alone. I pray for [fill in your name], who will believe in me through their message."

Let that thought penetrate deep. When Jesus was facing His cross, you were on His mind. He had your family, your needs, your mission, your giftedness, your purpose, and your heartaches, fears, successes, and joy on His mind. He prayed for you: "That all of them may be one, Father, just as you are in me and I am in you. May they also be in us so that the world may believe that you have sent me."

Jesus prayed for us to share oneness, or intimacy, with one another and with Him! Why? So that the world will believe that God sent Jesus and that Jesus loves the world. Our intimacy with God is our testimony!

What is so special about this oneness? Love! Jesus in essence was saying this, "We've longed to reconnect with them ever since their rejection separated us from one another. Now I am the Connector. I'm connecting them to You through Me!"

Jesus fulfilled the work God gave Him to do, and today you and I remain in this sin-stained shadow life to continue the work He began. We participate in the ministry of connecting others to our Father. We do this by living our lives as walking, talking, living, breathing testimonies of His love and His power.

> When Jesus was facing His cross, you were on His mind.

If you are not living in oneness with God, His power is not flowing through your life. If His power is not flowing through your life, you are not doing the work He commissioned you to do.

Your intimacy with God is your testimony.

Apart from intimacy and oneness with God and with one another we cannot possibly bring glory to God. We cannot make Him known to the world. "I have given them the glory that you gave me, that they may be one as we are one: I in them and you in me. May they be brought to complete unity to let the world know that you sent me and have loved them even as you have loved me" (John 17:22–23).

The Closing: John 17:24–26

Jesus closed His prayer by expressing His love for the disciples. You can almost taste the salty tears that most likely streamed down His cheeks as He expressed His grief over leaving His companions. Read John 17:24–26.

The main purpose of prayer is to draw us into oneness with God. Jesus prayed for us to experience this oneness. Today we pray so that we can develop this oneness.

Oh God, Please . . .

If you are reading this book with a group of friends, use the following to guide a time of prayer. If you are reading this book alone, consider journaling as you follow the prayer guide.

Think of a time you were especially intimate with someone—a friend, your mother or father, a child, perhaps your spouse. Where were you? What were you doing? Why did you feel so close at that moment?

1. Thank God for that person.
   (Just say, "Thank You, Lord, for _____.)

2. Thank God for that time.

3. Tell God you realize that He wants to have special times with you.

4. Tell Him you want that too.

5. Thank Him for Jesus' death. (Without Jesus' death that intimacy would be impossible.)

6. Thank God for loving you so much that He wants to move from your heart's religious place to its intimate place. Invite Him into that part of your heart that houses your most cherished relationships.

When I shared with Tom (my husband) that I used our dating relationship and marriage to illustrate the power of intimacy in prayer, Tom made this statement: "You can have time without intimacy, but you can't have intimacy without time."

Your intimacy with God will grow in direct proportion to the amount of time you put into reading God's Word and talking with Him. Tom and I are close because we spend time together. We talk daily. We talk sometimes for hours!

Pray: *Lord, I want to develop intimacy with You, and I understand that it will take time. Please wake me up early or keep me up late so that we can spend quality time together. I want to do whatever it takes to build intimacy with You. Lord, You have been . . . [To close your prayer time, say out loud a name that describes who God is to you. If you are praying with a group, take turns and then one person close.] Amen*

CHAPTER 5

Into Me See

David asked the men standing near him, "What will be done for the man who kills this Philistine and removes this disgrace from Israel? Who is this uncircumcised Philistine that he should defy the armies of the living God?"

— 1 SAMUEL 17:26

Thus far I've shared that prayer is the way we develop intimacy with God. Together we've taken a slow walk through John 17 and discovered that Jesus prayed that we will be one with God. By now you know that your intimacy with God is your testimony to the world. So before we move on, let's take one more look at what intimacy with God looks like.

What Is Intimacy with God?

I was asking God this question when I remembered someone saying that the word *intimacy* sounds a lot like "into me see."

Think about that. *Into me see.*

When I think of the most intimate human relationships I've experienced, the ones that I celebrate most are those where I have been privileged to bear my soul—to share my deepest dreams, fears, disappointments, failures, and success-es—and in the sharing I've experienced acceptance, encouragement, and love.

Into me see.

When I consider the most intimate relationships I've experienced on earth, I realize that I have been privileged to have been trusted with others' deepest dreams, fears, disappointments, failures, and successes—and in the sharing I've been honored to be trusted with such treasures.

Into me see.

It is an overwhelming thought that the Creator of the universe desires intimacy with me.

Why does He want that? I haven't got a clue. It's kind of like the baffling expression on the faces of my seminary roommates when I chose Tom. (I told you a little bit about our dating relationship, but I left out the part of the story that included multiple breakups and countless tears.)

> Your intimacy with God is your testimony to the world.

The other day I was eating lunch with my daughter Kaleigh and her friend from college. Kaleigh told me that she wasn't fond of another friend's boyfriend. I considered that a perfect teachable moment and proceeded to share my vast wisdom with these two adorable young women. "You know, that is something to consider," I said. "If your friends don't like your boyfriend, you should let that be a little flag. Maybe you don't have to break up with him over it, but it should be taken seriously and you should pray through it. Sometimes your emotions can play tricks on you, and you cannot see what your friends might see."

Kaleigh and her friend graciously accepted my advice. Then Kaleigh asked, "Mom, what did your friends think about Dad when you were dating him?"

Oops. I choked on my pita bread and laughed out loud. For the truth be known, my friends were not fond of him at all! They warned us not to get married. We took the Prepare/

Enrich marriage test and failed. Of course Kaleigh and her friend found this just as hilarious as I did, and we had a good hard laugh at my attempt to share my wisdom.

Tom broke up with me on several occasions and literally broke my heart, but I was smitten with him and took him back as often as he returned. My obvious love affair with pain baffled my roommates.

As I am baffled with God's.

For God So Loves

God's love for us makes no sense at all. We took what He entrusted to us and sold it for a bite of fruit. Then we started killing one another out of jealousy, and we adulterated ourselves so that by the time the earth was only a few years old, God was already sorry He made us (see Genesis 6:6).

> God wants a dynamic personal relationship with you.

But even God's grief didn't suspend His love. God loves you, and in His reckless abandon of ridiculous love He offered His very own Son to pay the penalty of sin just so He could draw you near to Himself. God longs for intimacy with you. He wants a dynamic (active and developing) personal (into me see) relationship with you.

If you do not know God personally, let me assure you, God knows you personally. He knows how many hairs are on your head; He has collected every tear you have ever shed. In heaven right now a precious collection of beautiful jars has your name on them. If you are a crier like me, you have quite the collection gathered there!

God loves you.

In fact, He loves you so much that while you were not even aware of Him—while you were still sinning and living for yourself—God sent His own Son, Jesus, to die in your place. Romans 6:23 says, "The wages of sin is death." Jesus took the wages your sin earned and stepped in to rescue you from death. He died so that you can live. Jesus paid for your sin when He willingly suffered on the cross.

You enter into an intimate place with God by receiving the precious gift of forgiveness that He offers you through the splintery, sin-stained, blood-soaked cross where Jesus died. It's simple really:

Believe . . . that God sent Jesus to die in your place.

Agree . . . with God that the only thing you bring to Him is the sin that nailed Jesus to the cross. Then . . .

Ask . . . the holy, perfect God to forgive you of your sins, and invite Him into your life—not only to take you to heaven when you die but to rule with heavenly authority while you continue to live the rest of your days here.

Romans 10:9–10 says, "That if you confess with your mouth, 'Jesus is Lord,' and believe in your heart that God raised him from the dead, you will be saved." But my friends, that is merely the "jumping on place." Once you have experienced salvation—the initial coming together of you and God—you then have the privilege of sitting in His lap. And this changes everything.

Oh God, Please . . .

If you are reading this book with a group of friends, share your answers to the following statements and questions. If you are reading alone, think about your answers and jot them down in your journal.

1. Consider your most intimate friend. Describe your friendship and why you are able to be so close.

2. How do you feel about God's "tear collection"? Why does He want to be so intimately acquainted with you? When have you experienced intimacy with Him?

3. When did you experience God's love personally? Try to describe the difference between understanding God with your head and understanding Him with your heart.

Pray: [Take a few minutes to reflect on your own salvation.] *Oh God, thank You for inviting me to become intimately acquainted with You. Thank You for loving me, for being attentive to me, and for inviting me to walk more closely with You. I want to love You with my mind and my heart. Please continue to teach me how to do that. Amen*

CHAPTER 6

A Place in God's Lap

"The Lord who delivered me from the paw of the lion and the paw of the bear will deliver me from the hand of this Philistine." Saul said to David, "Go, and the Lord be with you."

— 1 SAMUEL 17:37

Chapter 5 ended with the image of God holding us in His lap, but what is the full meaning of sitting in God's lap? What does it actually look like? Why is it such a privilege?

What Sitting in the Lap of God Is and Is Not

One of my favorite Bible stories is that of David and Goliath. I love this story because I know what it's like to face some rather scary giants. I also love this story because David shows us what we can do with those giants when we understand the privilege we have of sitting in God's lap.

If you have your Bible with you, read this story in 1 Samuel 17 before you read the rest of this chapter.

The Israelite army was invited to sit in the lap of God, but they allowed their training, their intelligence, and their uniforms, weapons, and strategies to replace their privilege of intimacy with their Heavenly Father. So when Goliath shouted, they knew only one thing: that giant was way bigger than the training, weapons, and experience they brought to the battlefield that day.

That happens, you know. Some of us were fortunate enough to become Christians at a young age—I was eleven. Although I knew I needed God every step of the way, I grew in my understanding of people; I was given many opportunities to study God's Word and lead in a church; I was privileged to be educated; and I learned from the mistakes and successes of others. But if I'm not careful, I can serve God efficiently without having any interaction with Him.

People will call me a "Christian," and I'll wear the "team colors." For the most part, I can make it just fine as long as a Philistine giant doesn't show up on my battlefield. But when a giant steps in front of me—when he hovers over me and heckles me—I know deep inside that none of my training, and nothing I've ever done before, has prepared me for anything quite like this.

> When you sit in the lap of God, you see the things of this world from a different angle.

God allows giants in our lives so that He can teach us more about His power and His love, but we will never defeat them without learning the pleasure of sitting in His lap. Do you have a Goliath heckling you? Then thank God for the invitation to sit in His lap.

When you sit in the lap of God, you see the things of this world from a different angle. You see a king who can be convinced to send a little boy as the army's best against an enemy who is far superior in physical strength, mental edge, and battle experience. When you sit in the lap of God, you see a giant who can be killed with a river rock and a slingshot. When you sit in the lap of God, you discover an army that can be rallied to victory by a shepherd boy.

Come and sit with me in God's lap.

A Small Boy in a Giant World

I experienced a personal understanding of what this means several years ago at Disney World in Florida. We had taken our three children with us to the Southern Baptist Convention in Orlando. While Tom attended the meetings to "amen" the recommendation to boycott a certain theme park, I decided to take our children to said park and set up surveillance to make sure other conventioneers were sticking to the boycott.

Before we left the hotel room that morning, Tom said, "I don't like the idea of you going by yourself with all three of our children. Are you sure you can keep up with them?" He had always feared that we would lose a child at a theme park. When my parents took our daughters Mikel and Kaleigh to the same park when they were four and five, Tom worried the entire time that they'd lose them there.

I assured Tom that I could keep up with everyone and he had nothing to worry about.

I parked our rented minivan in Donald Duck's lot and covered our noses with sunscreen. As we were packing our water bottles, lip balm, and camera, I gave the children a lecture on what to do in the highly unlikely event that they got separated from me.

"There are a lot of people at the park today," I said. "It will be easy to lose me, and I don't want to get lost. So stay close to me the whole time! Don't get out of my sight. *If* you do get separated from me, stay put. Just stand still and I will find you. Don't move! Does everyone understand?"

"Yes, Mama, we know! We won't lose you!" they assured me.

At least a billion people were at the park that day. Probably three-quarters of the conventioneers plus another entire country's population were squeezing past one another on Main

Street. After we got off the monorail and began our magic journey through the kingdom, we went right away to my favorite ride, "It's a Small World," and enjoyed our float through the land of babies singing that little song.

The children were excited about the new Winnie the Pooh ride, so we then hurried over to that part of the park. To skip the long line, we decided to take advantage of Disney's FastPass system, which is an express-lane ticket we would use at a particular time later on in the day. After Mikel, Kaleigh, and I figured out the machine and got our tickets, we looked around to find other rides nearby. It was then I realized that five-year-old T.J. was not with us.

At first I thought, *He's just behind that family over there*, but when I looked he was not there. Then I thought, *Well, he's right around the corner at the water fountain, of course*. I looked at the water fountain, but he was not there.

Mikel and Kaleigh began to get scared; people were pushing and shoving back and forth, hundreds of people! I hollered out his name; no one answered. Mikel and Kaleigh started calling; no one answered. Other moms and dads looked at me with terror-filled eyes, and they, too, started calling out, "T.J.!" . . . Still, no answer.

People who realized what had happened asked me what he looked like. I choked out, "Long curls, blue shorts, and a white T-shirt." In my mind I thought, *That could describe 7,892 children in the park today!* I saw a family who all wore pink shirts with black lettering, "Porter," and I wished we'd been so smart.

There were so many people scurrying around like ants on an anthill that I was afraid I would lose Mikel and Kaleigh in my search for T.J., so I set them down right outside a gift shop and dared them to move a muscle. I didn't want to ask for help because that was like admitting he was gone, and I didn't want to admit he was gone!

"T.J.!"

My heart beat fast, and fear began to engulf me. I was shaking as I walked into the gift shop, stepped up to the counter, and heard myself ask, "What do you do when someone loses a child?"

It was like a dream, and this should have been happening to someone else. Perhaps I thought that if I spoke in third person I could somehow make this another mother's nightmare.

A man stepped out from behind the counter and said, "I'll help you find him!" He must have been an angel.

I described my son again, told the man his name, and told him where we'd been. He said I ought to retrace my steps back to It's a Small World, and he'd go look all around Winnie the Pooh. Mikel and Kaleigh stayed next to the wall outside the gift shop and took care of the crying.

As I went all the way back to our last ride, I calculated the amount of time he'd already been separated from us. It had been at least fifteen minutes. Milk cartons and postcards flashed through my mind. He had to be here somewhere. God wouldn't let this happen to me. These kinds of things happen all the time. Disney World is one of the worst places for children to be abducted! Who told me that? Why did they have to say that?

I was searching for my little boy. There were so many children everywhere! All the families were happy, but my son was gone. He wasn't anywhere. What was he thinking, all alone out there? What was happening to my little boy? I was supposed to take care of him! Oh God, please bring him back to me. T.J. was nowhere to be found, and another ten minutes sucked the life out of me.

As I made my way back to help Mikel and Kaleigh cry, a terrifying thought plowed through all the others: *I'm going to have to call Tom and tell him I lost our son! Even after he warned me not to lose them! I couldn't keep up with them! I let him get away!* I imagined sitting in a little room on one side of a table describing T.J. to the security personnel, telling what he was wearing, unable to even remember exactly which white T-shirt I'd put on him that morning. Did he have on sandals or tennis shoes? I couldn't remember!

Mikel and Kaleigh were still outside the gift shop. They were doing a good job with their assignment as they huddled together and cried. We sat and waited for another ten minutes at least. I was looking out at the masses of people walking toward their next adventure wondering if I could just turn the clock back to this morning in our hotel room when T.J. thought the Disney store at the mall was actually Disney World.

Suddenly, out of the crowd came one little boy, with my angel behind him. When I saw T.J., I fell to my knees, cried out his name, and the minute he heard his name, he ran as fast as his little legs could carry him straight into my arms. I felt his heart beating as fast as mine as we embraced each other. And just as soon as he wrapped his arms around me, he took them away, stepped back, and placed his hands on both sides of my face. Then he said, "Mommy, oh Mommy!" as he looked deep into my eyes.

At that moment, my fears were washed away and T.J.'s salvation was complete. After we thanked the gift shop attendant for finding our boy, Mikel, Kaleigh, and I asked T.J. what happened. He said he never saw us walk over to the FastPass kiosk; he'd just kept walking. When he realized we weren't with him, he stood still just like I told him. But, he said, "Mommy, people were bumping into me! So I walked over to the side and waited. I know you told me to stay still, but they were walking into me! I just waited and I waited. I wasn't sure you were coming for me. Then this man said my name, and I knew he had to know me so I came with him and he brought me to you."

There are many spiritual lessons in this story, but the one I want to tell you about is this: I love my son, and my son loves me. When we were separated, I nearly lost my mind, and my world turned upside down. The air seemed harder to breathe, and I was consumed with my love for him.

When he was separated from me, he tried to obey me—and he tried to believe me—but when I didn't come for what seemed like hours, he was afraid. When we found each other again, both our fears and longings were wiped away. In the place of the anxiety created by our separation came incredible relief and overwhelming joy! I could've held T.J. tight for twenty minutes and never let him breathe. But T.J. wanted to look me in the face; he wanted to drink in the reality of me and express his relief. He did this by taking my face in his hands and saying, "Mommy, oh Mommy!" as he looked in my tear-filled eyes.

That, my friends, is a picture of what it is like to sit in your Father's lap. God draws you near to Himself!

Our Inheritance

God came down from heaven to find you. He came to seek and to save that which was lost. You were lost in your sin—left to yourself you were hopeless and helpless. But God in His infinite mercy came down to where you were, and He demonstrated His own love for you in that while you were still steeped in sin Christ died for you. God picked you up out of a sin-stained world and placed you in His lap.

Anytime I feel an overwhelming need for my Father's undivided attention, I can reach my hands to His face, hold it in my grasp, look Him in the eyes, and exclaim, "Daddy, oh Daddy!"

David defeated Goliath with a slingshot and a stone because he sat in the lap of God. From that viewpoint, David saw Goliath the way God saw Goliath—easily defeated, an enemy of the Lord!

If we are going to take on the giants in our world today, we *must* spend time in the lap of God. Paul urged us to do this: "Because those who are led by the Spirit of God are sons of God. For you did not receive a spirit that makes you a slave again to fear, but you received the Spirit of sonship. And by him we cry, 'Abba, Father.' The Spirit Himself testifies with our spirit that we are God's children. Now if we are children, then we are heirs—heirs of God and co-heirs with Christ, if indeed we share in his sufferings in order that we may also share in his glory" (Romans 8:14–17).

Daddy! God!

> If we are going to take on the giants in our world today, we *must* spend time in the lap of God.

The word *Abba* literally means, "Daddy." It's more than a title; it's a relationship. Prior to Jesus dying for our sins, this title would have never been considered appropriate for man to use when referring to Jehovah God. When Jesus was praying in the garden of Gethsemane, He went beyond the more formal "Father" to an intimate, taking-His-Father's-face-in-His-hands-beseeching plea: "Abba! Father! All things are possible for You; remove this cup from Me; yet not what I will, but what You will" (Mark 14:36 NASB).

"Daddy, oh Daddy!"

Jesus came to share sonship with us. Paul said, "The Spirit Himself testifies with our spirit that we are children of God, and if children, heirs also, heirs of God and fellow heirs with Christ" (Romans 8:16–17 NASB).

Oh God, Please . . .

1. Does my story trigger one of your own? Have you ever had a sitting-in-the-lap-of-God experience? If so, share that with your group. If you are reading this book alone, ask God to give you someone with whom you can share your story.

2. Are you facing a giant in your life today? What does your giant look like? What part of that giant causes you fear?

3. Crawl up into the lap of God by reading Psalm 145 out loud. Now look at your giant again. Is your God bigger? Can your giant be defeated? Thank God for the victory that is yours today.

Pray: *Thank You, Lord, for inviting me to not only draw near to Your throne of grace but also to crawl right up into Your lap. Thank You for Jesus' blood that makes this kind of intimacy possible. Help me to gain Your perspective on the giants I'm facing today. Let me be reminded that nothing is impossible with You. Amen*

CHAPTER 7

How Do I Do That, Really?

David said to the Philistine, "You come against me with sword and spear and javelin, but I come against you in the name of the Lord Almighty, the God of the armies of Israel, whom you have defied. This day the Lord will hand you over to me, and I'll strike you down and cut off your head. Today I will give the carcasses of the Philistine army to the birds of the air and the beasts of the earth, and the whole world will know that there is a God in Israel."

— 1 SAMUEL 17:45-46

Most likely you don't tend sheep for a living, as David of the Old Testament did, so you don't have alone time built into your day when you can rest against a rock and strum on your harp. As a youngster David had an advantage over us, but later on in his life, he had trouble maintaining his lap-sitting posture with God. When life got a bit busier, he neglected this time and got himself into all kinds of trouble.

This is a reminder that we can't live today on yesterday's lap. God wants us to sit with Him daily. Intimacy does not happen automatically, nor is intimacy developed instantaneously. We must work at developing intimacy in any relationship, including the relationship we have with God. But how are we supposed to develop intimacy with God in the midst of the hustle and bustle of our lives?

Intimacy Develops over Time

My husband and I dated for many months before we felt safe enough to begin to allow the other a glimpse of "into me see." And even after we married, the intimacy we share today, twenty-five years into our life together, is much greater than that which we shared after only five years of marriage. Our intimacy has grown through

> God wants us to sit with Him daily.

the circumstances we've experienced together, including infertility treatment, pregnancies, and the births of our three children; the tragic death of my husband's brother; weathering a difficult division in our congregation; more deaths of loved ones; Tom's doctorate; our children's first breakups, ball games, and ignorant coaches; burying church members' babies; enjoying vacations; and sharing the gospel in China—the list could go on and on and on. If this human relationship that I have with a man who baffled my seminary roommates can grow to be this intimate, how much more potential there is for *intimacy* in my relationship with a God who knows me best and loves me most!

Your intimacy with God will develop with time. Some of the time you spend with God will be structured; some will not. During your structured time, take the initiative to be still. Turn off the television. (Have you been listening to talk show hosts more than the voice of God?) Get out of bed earlier. Put down that book. Shut off your computer. Do whatever you have to do to spend *time* with God.

You cannot experience intimacy with God without spending time with God, and the time you spend with God will not come easy. There is nothing your enemy would rather you do less than spend time with God.

During the time you spend, read God's Word; listen for His voice; and invite Him to direct your day. I will talk more about this later, but rest in this truth: if you will set aside time and read God's Word in a systematic way, God will speak to you. He knows better how to communicate with you than you know how to communicate with Him. If you don't know how to pray, invite God to teach you.

Intimacy Develops in a One-on-one Relationship

My husband and I would not be quite as intimate with each other if we always took our vacations with extended family. In order for us to share intimacy, we have to put aside *time with each other*. And let me tell you this, I do not want someone else to describe my relationship with Tom. I do not want others telling me how they talk to him, encouraging me to enjoy him the way they are able to enjoy him. That is crazy!

> If you will set aside time and read God's Word in a systematic way, God will speak to you.

But don't we do that sometimes? Maybe you don't watch talk shows on television; maybe you listen to Bible teachers on the radio. Even if you are listening to great, doctrinally sound biblical scholars, you don't need to substitute their time with God for your own. And maybe you don't read romance novels; you complete every fill-in-the-blank Bible study you can get your hands on. Don't get me wrong. I love Bible studies (I've written five and hope to write more soon), but please understand this: it is best to use Bible studies only as tools to help you get into God's Word for yourself!

You can have intimacy with God. You don't have to receive it secondhand. Your intimacy with God will develop in a one-on-one relationship.

Intimacy with God Grows in Community

While there is no substitute for the time you will spend alone with God, there is also no way to live in the fullness of intimacy with God without the others in your world. Your intimacy with God will grow when you allow yourself to love other believers. Your intimacy with God will grow when you allow other believers to love you. This is called "church"! Jesus endorsed this kind of "into me see" in John 17:20–23. You will recall we discussed these verses in previous chapters.

> Spiritual warfare is meant to be fought with platoons not mercenaries.

Our intimacy with God grows in community with others.

Consider the story of David and Goliath. The story didn't end when Goliath fell. Read 1 Samuel 17:50–53. David's victory over Goliath rallied the troops. His intimacy with God reminded the Israelite army that they belonged to the Almighty, the God of Israel.

Your intimacy with God will do the same. Faith is contagious, and spiritual warfare is meant to be fought with platoons not mercenaries.

Intimacy with God
Proclaims God's Name to the World

David had one goal in mind when he stood before Goliath. Some readers miss this, but please don't be one who does. Read 1 Samuel 17:45–46. David's goal went beyond decapitating Goliath. According to verse 46, David was eager for the world to know God like he knew God.

Do you know God like David knew God? Do you want the world to know God like you know God?

Several years ago on a Tuesday night, Sumer and Corey came to our house for dinner. I'd invited them because I wanted to hear Sumer tell me her story. Her mother and father had died in a plane crash when she was eleven years old. She and her brother then lived with their grandmother, and although they were orphans they both grew in their relationships with the Lord.

Now skip briefly to years later when one January Sumer (who served on our church staff in the preschool ministry) went with two of our other preschool ministers to Africa on a mission trip to visit orphans. She anticipated this trip because she sensed God talking to her about a new plan He had for her life, but the conversation between her and God hadn't begun with a call to Africa—it had started with a challenge to give Him her dreams.

Sumer told me that the first time God challenged her to surrender her dreams to Him was when she was a student in college. She explained that way back then she dreamed of marrying, having children, and owning a home. In essence she wanted what many of us want; Sumer wanted to enjoy a family and a career. Once she put her dreams into words and presented them to God, He challenged her to let Him have them—to release them to Him. As a young college student,

Sumer told God that she trusted Him to do in her life what-ever He wished, and she would gladly follow Him.

Life moved forward. God allowed her to marry, have three children, own a home, and enjoy her career. Before Sumer worked with us, she taught statistics at Belmont University. It was after the move to our church staff that God came back to her and asked her to give Him her dreams once again.

She explained that this time it was more difficult. It was one thing to give God her dreams before they came true but a bit harder when they were sitting in front of her.

Nevertheless she and her husband put their house on the market. Sumer said that it wasn't terribly difficult to give God her husband and children—what ownership did she have over them anyway? But her house? That was what she actually owned. It was what she loved and what made her life stable. But Sumer explained that she felt like God asked her specifi-cally to give Him her home.

The night we were eating dinner a "for sale" sign was in front of Sumer and Corey's house. In January Sumer went to Africa—eager to see if God might further reveal Himself to her there.

It wasn't until her team visited Korah that she heard God's voice again. Korah houses the city dump, and nearly one hun-dred children were living there, foraging for their "daily bread." Few mission teams ever ventured to the dump. Its stench, filth, and poverty were too much even for the brave-hearted souls who journeyed to Africa on mission. One of my other friends confessed to me that it literally made her sick; she couldn't wait to get out of there.

Sumer, however, came alive in the dump. Sumer sat in the lap of God while in Korah's dump. As she watched those chil-dren eat from garbage (many of them orphans), she saw them from God's point of view.

Today Sumer, Corey, and their three young sons live in Ethiopia and minister to more than two hundred children who once lived in Korah. Hundreds of people in our church (and in other churches) sponsor those children, who are now enrolled in a boarding school far away from the city dump and far away from lives of despair. Hundreds of other people travel to Africa many times each year to join Sumer and Corey in their mission. In fact just recently a team of nineteen left for Korah so "the whole world will know that there is a God."

Intimacy with God proclaims God's name to the world.

Only God can take a young woman like Sumer, who was orphaned at eleven and later lived in a small dot on the map in suburbia Tennessee, and connect her to the orphaned children who lived in a dump in Ethiopia. Sumer's intimacy with God took her there.

God allowed Sumer to suffer the loss of her parents, but out of the ashes He brought beauty. And I am here to confess that the happiest person at our table that Tuesday night was Sumer! The evidence of her intimacy with God radiated in her face as she shared with us her plans for the children of Korah.

God longs for intimacy with you. He might not send you to Africa—but He might. And if He does, it's because Africa is His gift to you! He might send you next door—or across the street or downtown. But I'm sure of this: when you develop your intimacy with God, He's going to send you somewhere to share His love with someone. Because as much as God longs for intimacy with you, He also longs for intimacy with others who don't even know Him yet.

Oh God, Please . . .

1. If you don't already have a time set aside to meet God by reading His Word, schedule that time now. I will meet God [when] _____ and [where] _____. Share with one another the times you have set for yourself.

2. Many great tools can assist you in your time with God. Some of my favorites are daily devotional books such as the classics *Streams in the Desert* and *My Utmost for His Highest*. I also enjoy a devotional Bible that provides daily Scripture readings such as the *Chronological Daily Bible* and the *Prayer Devotional Bible*. What are some of your favorite quiet time tools?

3. Another tool that I encourage you to use is a journal. It is helpful to jot down the thoughts you are having and the impressions you are receiving when you sit with God. Even printing a verse of Scripture on paper helps you absorb its truth. Share how you use a journal in your quiet time.

4. Try different tools until you find the ones that work best for you. But commit now to set aside the time and place to meet with God on a daily basis, and do whatever you have to do to keep that commitment. As is true in any relationship, your intimacy will develop with whatever time and effort you invest in it.

Pray: *Father, we want to crawl into Your lap right now. As we worship You, we want to look full in Your wonderful face. Daddy, oh Daddy! Thank You for saving us. Grow us in our relationship with You—and let us live resting in the simple warmth of Your good pleasure. Thank You for loving us first. Amen*

PART 2

Prayer Is . . . a Privilege

Prayer should not be regarded as a duty which must be performed, but rather as a privilege to be enjoyed, a rare delight that is always revealing some new beauty.

—

E. M. BOUNDS

CHAPTER 8

A Holy Place in Life

Therefore, brothers, since we have confidence to enter the Most Holy Place by the blood of Jesus, by a new and living way opened for us through the curtain, that is, his body, and since we have a great priest over the house of God, let us draw near to God with a sincere heart in full assurance of faith, having our hearts sprinkled to cleanse us from a guilty conscience and having our bodies washed with pure water.

— HEBREWS 10:19–22

In 1995 Tom and I were given a trip to Israel. Although I was reluctant to leave my young children behind with my mother (I had to wean T.J. in order to go), I have to confess that it was an experience I will never forget. If you ever have the opportunity to visit the Holy Land, take it!

Tom and I shared a private joke about the Department of Tourism while we were in Israel. Often our tour guide took us to what he said was the "exact place where . . . ." We would look around the area and wonder, *Now how does he know that?* Nevertheless, because the crusaders built sacred buildings over them, many of the holy places have been well preserved even amidst constant war.

Because of those preservation efforts and because the layers of life pile on top of one another, we had to walk down into many basements to cast our gaze on the "exact locations where . . ." But the one I want to tell you about now is the dark basement tunnel we walked through to see a massive rock located underneath the hill called Golgotha. The rock has a visible crack through its middle that is presumed to be a result of the earthquake that shook the earth when Jesus breathed His last.

> Today we can boldly go where no human could go prior to Jesus' death on the cross.

At the same time, Scripture tells us, the curtain of the temple was torn from top to bottom. The temple curtain had separated ordinary people from the Most Holy Place, which represented the presence of God. You and I would have never been allowed to go beyond that curtain. Some of the priests were allowed behind the veil but only on certain occasions, and never without having a string tied to their ankles in case God slayed them and they had to be pulled out from His presence.

When Jesus died on the cross, the veil that separated the people from the Most Holy Place was torn in two: "At that moment the curtain of the temple was torn in two from top to bottom. The earth shook and the rocks split" (Matthew 27:51). When God ripped the veil, He declared the separation of man and God removed. Sin separates us from God, but Jesus' death paid sin's price and purchased our salvation. So today we can boldly go where no human could go prior to Jesus' death on the cross. Today, we can go boldly to the throne of grace where Jesus' blood paves our way.

By the time you complete this book, I want you to have a sober appreciation of this incredible privilege.

A Strange Story

If you have your Bible (and I hope you do), then read 2 Samuel 6:1–15 before I give you a quick retelling here.

After David experienced great success as a warrior and was well established as king, he took thirty thousand of his men and set out to fetch the ark of God, the Old Testament equivalent to the Holy of Holies. The ark of God represented the presence of God, and because David understood its significance and appreciated its value, he had it placed on a brand new cart pulled by oxen.

The ark had been at the house of Abinadab, and two of his sons, Uzzah and Ahio, went with the ark and David's men. In fact, Scripture tells us that Ahio and Uzzah actually guided the cart that carried the precious cargo. As they followed behind, David and all thirty thousand of his men celebrated—singing and playing harps, lyres, tambourines, sistrums (whatever those are), and cymbals. I imagine that this was quite the parade!

> Holiness cannot tolerate sin—not even when the person stained by it does something with good intent.

Along the way, however, the oxen stumbled, and Uzzah reached out his hand to steady the ark (and keep it from falling) . . . and the heavens opened wide, angels began to sing, and Uzzah was honored for his quick hands and thoughtful action. Is that what your Bible says? It's kind of what I think it should say, but according to 2 Samuel 6:7 that is not at all what happened: "The Lord's anger burned against Uzzah because of his irreverent act; therefore God struck him down and he died there beside the ark of God."

Wait, did we read that right? You mean to tell me that Uzzah kept the ark from falling off that cart, and rather than be blessed, God killed him?! I don't get it. And neither did David: "Then David was angry because the Lord's wrath had broken out against Uzzah" (2 Samuel 6:8a).

When I read this story, I feel a bit like David—I'm baffled by God's severe punishment against Uzzah for doing what I consider a good deed. He was trying to keep the ark of God from falling off the ox cart!

But, the holiness of God is just that: holy. (*Holiness* is another word for flawlessness, for something "not blemished by sin," for something "set apart and perfect in every way.")

Well-meaning Uzzah was still stained by sin, and when sin touched the ark of God (which represented the presence of God's holiness), sin was destroyed. That's what holiness does. Perfection destroys imperfection. Holiness cannot tolerate sin—not even when the person stained by it does something with good intent.

We forget this sometimes. We've grown so complacent—so accepting—so soft on sin, and so accustomed to and maybe even presumptuous of grace that we forget what holiness is.

On Facebook a friend of mine posted some lyrics from a popular country song, and I was disheartened to see several other young girls whom I love indicate they "liked" her post. Basically, the song touted a wild life and expressed pride in being bad. Most of the girls who responded on the social networking site are seeking God in their lives today. Some of them have made mistakes that resulted in the blessing of babies, and they are eager to be good mothers. While I appreciate the grace my friend is experiencing as she tries to make sense of where she is today, the song's lyrics take grace beyond its borders. Don't be proud of your mistakes, and please don't celebrate that you broke the rules.

Uzzah died because David didn't seek God's instructions on how to move His ark. Had David taken the time to honor God's instructions, Uzzah would not have died. David would have known that God's ark should never be placed on an ox cart in the first place. God had given the Israelites specific instructions on how to transport His ark. According to those instructions, God's ark should have been carried on poles by Levites who had gone through a ceremonial cleansing process.

Holiness is the fundamental nature of God. We've lost a healthy appreciation of God's holiness today. Yes, if you have accepted Jesus' death on the cross as the substitute for punishment you deserved for your sin, then you are welcome in the presence of a holy God. But those doors do not stand wide open on the merit of your good deeds, your great worship, your discipline, or even your humility.

> Holiness is the fundamental nature of God.

The doors to the throne room of God were pushed open in a tidal wave of blood, blood that flowed from the splintered beam of a Roman fixture of torture. And lest we take the cross of Jesus for granted, just let the images of crucifixion pour through your mind's eyes.

Those things you did that broke your mama's heart nailed Jesus to the cross. The hell you raised actually mocked Him as He strained to breathe. Yes, mistakes lead us to the cross, and, yes, God forgives everyone. But NO, please don't ever be proud of those mistakes, and please don't ever celebrate the part you played in the beating Jesus took to set you free.

Was it the ripping of His beard that covered your night out? Or was it the spit that ran down His cheek? Maybe it was the seventeenth lash of the thirty-nine He suffered. Remember? The lashes that ripped His skin to shreds and paid for the lies, the theft, the drunkenness, and the immorality you participated in.

Who celebrates sin? Don't ever let it be a precious, privileged child of the King.

Do come boldly to the throne of grace. Know that your Savior not only welcomes you there but He also beckons you to come. Walk softly, though, for the way is paved with the blood of Jesus and you come on the merit of His sinless life—of His perfect sacrifice—and of His obedience to His Father and the love They both have for you.

Oh God, Please . . .

1. Remember my mention of that country song's lyrics, how it tried to make the bad life seem good? Ask God if there are times when your attitude toward sin has been flippant.

2. Ask God to give you a right understanding of sin and a sober reminder of the price tag connected with it. Share a specific image of Jesus' suffering that comes to your mind.

> **Pray:** *Lord, thank You for loving me when I was at my worst. Help me to never forget the price You paid to forgive my sin. I'm sorry for [be specific] . . . Thank You for Your forgiveness, for grace, and for mercy. I love You, Lord, and want to give my life to You in gratitude for all that You've given me. In Jesus' precious, powerful, and holy name I pray. Amen*

CHAPTER 9

A Lesson Learned in a Hindu Temple

"You are worthy, our Lord and God, to receive glory and honor and power, for you created all things, and by your will they were created and have their being."

— REVELATION 4:11

When I went to India, I waded through a Hindu temple. It was an experience I will never forget.

After walking through a fair-type atmosphere where booths were set up and crowds of people were purchasing trinkets and food and holy powders, our group was taken to a place where we were told to shed our shoes. The Hindu worshippers wanted us to take off our socks, too, but we couldn't bring ourselves to do that. You see, India overall is a dirty place, and this Hindu temple was no exception. The ground was covered with leftover food, paper, and all kinds of garbage tossed down with no regard whatsoever for keeping litter in its place, much less recycling.

Sock footed, we followed the worshippers as they stood in a line waiting to enter their version of the Holy of Holies for one of their many gods, Ganesh. They brought powders and confetti to toss toward the his golden image, but some of them started tossing their worship before they ever got to Ganesh. Temple attendants carried buckets of water and brooms, and they poured the water on the ground and then used the brooms to sweep the area clean. I suppose they did this so that each of the worshipper's powders and confetti would have a chance of being at the top of the heap for only a minute of Ganesh's

precious time—that is, *if* he was awake. More temple attendants stood by bells that were hanging just at the entrance to his "throne," and they struck the bells with a rod in case Ganesh needed to be roused from his rest.

When I think of the throne room of God, I think of a much different place. I need no magic powder or confetti to sprinkle before Him. I am not driven there by fear of what God might do to me if I don't worship Him properly. I am not assured of prosperity and blessing simply because I show up and give Him homage.

> We would do well to enter the holy dwelling of the God ever aware of the warm flow of Jesus' blood that paves our way there.

And when I come, I don't need bells to awaken Him. God never sleeps (see Psalm 121:4), and He certainly isn't some cold, gold statue that sits lifeless on His throne. John describes the throne room of God in Revelation 4:

> *At once I was in the Spirit, and there before me was a throne in heaven with someone sitting on it. And the one who sat there had the appearance of jasper and carnelian. A rainbow, resembling an emerald, encircled the throne. Surrounding the throne were twenty-four other thrones, and seated on them were twenty-four elders. They were dressed in white and had crowns of gold on their heads. From the throne came flashes of lightning, rumblings and peals of thunder. Before the throne, seven lamps were blazing. These are the seven spirits of God. Also before the throne there was what looked like a sea of glass, clear as crystal. (vv. 2–6a)*

The description of the throne room of God continues and only gets better, but there is one part of my experience in Ganesh's throne room that might be valuable to relate to the throne room of God. When I visited Ganesh, I waded through a wet layer of worship powders, confetti, and I don't even want to imagine what else. When I enter the throne room of God, the floor is covered with the sweet, precious, life-giving blood of Jesus Christ.

We would do well to enter the holy dwelling of the Lord God Almighty ever aware of the warm flow of Jesus' blood that paves our way there. We must not take this privilege for granted and for one instant forget that although it is free it cost Jesus all that He had to give.

Freedom Is Not Free

My son-in-law joined the army, and after many weeks he graduated from basic training. The parts of his uniform all mean something, but one part that hangs on his neck sobers me more than the others. Every soldier who guards our freedom wears two dog tags. These tags have their name, social security number, and blood type punched on them. The small one is the toe tag, which hangs off the main chain and is linked with 52 beads. The large tag hangs on the neck chain that is linked with 365 beads. These beads are strategically designed as a type of calendar; if the soldier becomes a prisoner of war, he or she can break the chain and use the beads to keep up with time.

Our soldiers wear these dog tags as a constant reminder that they are willing to give their very lives for our freedom.

A few years ago I was invited to Germany to host a prayer clinic for our troops stationed there. I visited the Vogelweh Army Post and Ramstein Air Force Base. Ramstein is the home of the 86th Airlift Division that serves Landstuhl Regional Medical Center, which is the largest military hospital outside the US. Soldiers who are injured in battle are flown to the Ramstein base and treated at Landstuhl.

As I visited this small piece of America planted in the middle of Europe, I was sobered by the price of my freedom. I felt a deep appreciation not only for the men and women in uniform who wear those dog tags and put their lives in harm's way but also for the husbands, wives, and children they leave behind to do their jobs. Most Americans go about their business on a daily basis rarely ever thinking about the sacrifices that are being made to secure for them life, liberty, and the pursuit of happiness.

> God sent His own Son to suffer and die for no other reason than that He chose to love us.

Our freedom is not free; it's costly—just ask any wife of any soldier how much our freedom costs her. But somewhere along the way, she and her soldier-husband committed their lives to serve us. They considered the cost and chose to pay it. Most likely they had their reasons, and I've romanticized this a bit. Their reasons might have had a whole lot more to do with what worked for them than what was being given to us. Nevertheless we benefit from their sacrifices.

Our free access to the throne of God is not free either. Unlike any soldier who serves the land of the "free and the brave," God sent His own Son to suffer and die for no other reason than that He chose to love us.

Prayer is a privilege that we ought not take for granted.

A Coveted Position

Just one more thing I want to say about the privilege we have to enter the throne room of God. If you are keeping your Bible close as you read this book, start flipping the pages way back toward the beginning and find Exodus 33. I first heard David Platt make this great observation in the Scripture I'm about to share with you.

> *Now Moses used to take a tent and pitch it outside the camp some distance away, calling it the "tent of meeting." Anyone inquiring of the Lord would go to the tent of meeting outside the camp. And whenever Moses went out to the tent, all the people rose and stood at the entrances to their tents, watching Moses until he entered the tent. As Moses went into the tent, the pillar of cloud would come down and stay at the entrance, while the Lord spoke with Moses. Whenever the people saw the pillar of cloud standing at the entrance to the tent, they all stood and worshiped, each at the entrance to his tent. The Lord would speak to Moses face to face, as a man speaks with his friend. Then Moses would return to the camp, but his young aide Joshua son of Nun did not leave the tent. (Exodus 33:7–11)*

This is what a prayer meeting looked like in its earliest days. Only one man, Moses, got to actually attend the meeting. All the other people watched him as he went. I wonder what they might have been thinking. Because they stood at the entrances of their tents looking toward the tent of meeting, I have to assume they were longing to be there with

Moses. Most likely they wondered what it might be like to get to be beyond that cloud pillar and meet God face to face.

The Israelites saw God at a distance and wanted to be up close and personal. They longed to have an audience with God, but instead they were kept at bay. So they watched and waited and anticipated what they might learn from Moses' meeting with God.

Moses' tent of meeting didn't have a state-of-the art sound system, nor did it have large screens hanging on the curtained walls where the prayer meeting participants could enjoy PowerPoint presentations. No, the Israelites had none of this. Instead they had a pillar-shaped cloud that settled over the entrance to a tent, and they all stopped what they were doing and attended the prayer meetings.

Compare their priority of prayer to the priority we place on prayer today. Unlike them, we have full access to much more than a tent of meeting. We have the actual *throne room of God!* We are not only welcome to enter in but God Himself invites us to join Him!

I still remember the profound moment in my own prayer life when I realized that God is the One who waits on me to come to Him. I don't know about you, but when I go to the Vanderbilt Walk-in Clinic four miles south of here, I wait for the medical professionals to see me. One day Kaleigh and I waited for them for three hours. Maybe it's just me, but when I'm sitting in a waiting room, I can't help but think, *Why is their time more important than mine? Are they more important than me? Why should I sit and wait while they work?*

Now transition that way of thinking to God. Here is the *Creator* of the universe,

> We are not only welcome to enter in but God Himself invites us to join Him!

the Supreme Being, the *King of kings* and *Lord of lords*, waiting for me to come to Him just so He can be more intimately acquainted with me!

Prayer is a privilege. Don't miss it.

Oh God, Please . . .

Prayer is a privilege. And while we are urged to draw near to the throne of grace, we would do well to remember that our freedom to do so was paid with a price. Jesus gave all that He had so that we—who had nothing to give—could come anyway.

God loves you—so much so that He invites you to enter into a dynamic, intimate, and personal relationship with Him. You will experience the depth of this amazing relationship as you learn to pray.

To grow in your prayer life this week, set aside twenty minutes each day and read the various passages of Scripture that I've shared with you in chapters 8 and 9: Hebrews 10:19–22; Revelation 4:2–11; 2 Samuel 6:1–15; and Exodus 33:7–11. If you are participating in a group study, share how your prayer time has been impacted by what you are learning. Complete the following in your quiet time this week then share your experience with one another.

1. Before you read, pray this prayer: *Lord, show me what You want me to know from these verses.*

2. As you read, listen closely to your heart and see what parts of these verses seem to especially speak to you— perhaps they will remind you of something I said that made a significant impression on you.

3. Write that part of that verse down—or jot down the thought that you have.

4. Pray this prayer: *Lord, I want to honor You today by living in agreement with Your Word. How do You want me to apply this truth* [the truth God just revealed to you as you read] *to my life?* [The Holy Spirit will most likely direct your thoughts toward your actions, your attitudes, or your behaviors in relationship to people or circumstances in your life.]

5. Write down the thoughts you have in response to that prayer.

6. Thank God for speaking to you in His Word.

7. Continue listening for the voice of the Holy Spirit throughout the day. You might discover that as you are in the middle of a conversation you suddenly remember what you read in God's Word. That thought might relate to what you read today or yesterday or even the day before. As you anticipate hearing God's voice throughout your day, you will begin to recognize Him and soon you will discover that He talks to you all the time!

   A sober warning: Many other "voices" are out there. Most of them want to deceive you. There is only one voice of God. His voice will always line up with His Word. So, if you hear a voice and wonder if it is from God, be sure to test the thought with Scripture. We will discuss this more in the coming chapters.

Prayer is not a work that can be
allocated to one or another
group in the church.
It is everybody's responsibility;
it is everybody's privilege.

—

A. W. TOZER

PART 3

Prayer Is . . . Powerful

> Prayer breaks all bars, dissolves all chains,
> opens all prisons, and widens all straits
> by which God's saints have been held.
>
> —
>
> E. M. BOUNDS

CHAPTER 10

The Power of Prayer

"I tell you the truth, whatever you bind on earth will be bound in heaven, and whatever you loose on earth will be loosed in heaven. Again, I tell you that if two of you on earth agree about anything you ask for, it will be done for you by my Father in heaven. For where two or three come together in my name, there am I with them."

— MATTHEW 18:18–20

What a powerful promise. According to the above words from Matthew, if we are disciples of Christ, we have spiritual authority. This authority includes binding and loosing spiritual powers of darkness, and our power increases when we pray with kindred spirits.

I don't know about you, but I rarely meet evangelical Christians who operate with a sense of authority. Most Christ followers who accompany me on life's journey spend much of their energy trying to cope with the dastardly deeds of darkness from the posture of helpless victims.

> Prayer's power flows out of the life of Christ.

What might life look like if you embraced the authority you have over darkness? As you develop your prayer life, you will grow in understanding the height and breadth of spiritual authority that belongs to you.

Praying in the Name of Jesus

Prayer's power flows out of the life of Christ. Just as Jesus' blood paves our way to God's throne, so His life-giving blood empowers our prayers.

If you grew up attending church prayer meetings, you no doubt heard people praying "in Jesus' name." Most often I heard that phrase spoken as a benediction to the prayer just before the "amen." It was kind of like a postage stamp licked and stuck to the prayer-letter as it was sent on its way to heaven. But I shudder to think how many times those words have closed prayers that did anything *but* reflect the name of Jesus.

> The name of Jesus has authority in your life when the nature of Jesus has priority in it.

Praying in Jesus' name means to pray by the authority of Jesus. Praying in Jesus' name means to pray in harmony with Jesus. And praying in Jesus' name means to pray prayers sanctioned by Jesus.

In the next few chapters, you will learn what is meant by praying with His authority, in harmony with Him, and praying prayers that He sanctions.

Praying by the Authority of Jesus

When you pray in Jesus' name, you pray with Jesus' authority and His power, but this authority and power are not released to anyone who can utter the words. To pray by the authority of Jesus is to submit to His lordship in your life.

When Jesus delivered the Sermon on the Mount, His message was different than anything His audience had ever heard before. Toward the end of the message, He exhorted listeners to take His words to heart. He warned them that they could go through their entire lives thinking they were followers of Christ only to discover in the end that true discipleship is much more than giving lip service to God.

> "Many will say to me on that day, 'Lord, Lord, did we not prophesy in your name, and in your name drive out demons and perform many miracles?' Then I will tell them plainly, 'I never knew you. Away from me, you evildoers!' Therefore everyone who hears these words of mine and puts them into practice is like a wise man who built his house on the rock. The rain came down, the streams rose, and the winds blew and beat against that house; yet it did not fall, because it had its foundation on the rock. But everyone who hears these words of mine and does not put them into practice is like a foolish man who built his house on sand. The rain came down, the streams rose, and the winds blew and beat against that house, and it fell with a great crash." (Matthew 7:22–27)

According to this warning, you can prophesy, drive out demons, and even perform miracles yet completely miss intimacy with Jesus.

I know people who allow their disappointment in others to stop them from having a personal relationship with God. This passage of Scripture addresses that barrier to belief. Even Jesus will reject those who claim to work in His name if they do not have a dynamic, intimate, personal relationship with

Him. If hypocrites live long enough, their own hypocrisy will be exposed.

The name of Jesus has authority in your life when the nature of Jesus has priority in your life. When you worship God in spirit and in truth and when you walk in obedience to His Word, Jesus' authority will validate your prayers and your ministry. It was this authority that astonished Jesus' audience that day on the mountainside: "When Jesus had finished this sermon, the crowds were astonished at His teaching, because He was teaching them like one who had authority, and not like their scribes" (Matthew 7:28–29 HCSB).

Jesus' teaching differed from the other teachings in His day. While others taught probabilities and theory, Jesus taught truth. He spoke "like one who had authority." Jesus taught like one who had authority because He was one who had authority.

Authority to Forgive Sins

Read Matthew 9:1–8. When Jesus arrived in His hometown, some men brought a paralytic to Him. When Jesus saw the faith of the paralyzed man's friends, He said to the paralytic, "Take heart, son; your sins are forgiven" (Matthew 9:2).

Some teachers of the law were standing near, and they scoffed at Jesus. Don't forget that He was in His own town. Most likely these religious leaders had known Jesus since He was a young boy. They'd watched Him grow up, and they knew of His ministry. Perhaps they were even looking for reason to give Him counsel.

What they didn't realize is that Jesus could read their minds, and because He knew what they were thinking, He seized a teachable moment. Remember in John 14:10 when Jesus told His disciples that the words He said were not His own, that they belonged to His Father? Remember what He said when He told them that? "The *words* I say to you are not just my own. Rather, it is the Father, living in me, who is doing his *work*" (italics added). Jesus talked about "words," then meshed His words right into His Father's "work." Because Jesus had authority, or power, to forgive sin, His actions illustrated the authority of His words.

And that is what He did with this paralytic man in His own hometown. Once Jesus knew the teachers were challenging His authority, He asked them a question: "Which is easier: to say, 'Your sins are forgiven,' or to say, 'Get up and walk'?" (Matthew 9:5). Then He answered His own question not with words but with work: "But so that you may know that the Son of Man has authority on earth to forgive sins . . ." Then He said to the paralytic, "Get up, take your mat and go home" (v. 6).

> When Jesus ministered, He ministered with authority. And the authority that Jesus had He passed on to us.

I like this next part best: "And the man got up and went home. When the crowd saw this, they were filled with awe; and they praised God, who had given such authority to men" (v. 8).

What did Jesus have that enabled Him to both forgive sin and heal this man? Authority.

What was His motive for healing this man? To demonstrate the authority He had to forgive sin.

Why were the crowds amazed? Because God had given authority to men: "When the crowds saw this, they were awestruck and gave glory to God who had given such authority to men" (Matthew 9:8 HCSB).

When Jesus taught, He taught with authority. When Jesus ministered, He ministered with authority. And the authority that Jesus had He passed on to us: "All authority in heaven and on earth has been given to me. Therefore go and make disciples of all nations, baptizing them in the name of the Father and of the Son and of the Holy Spirit, and teaching them to observe everything I have commanded you. And surely I am with you always, to the very end of the age" (Matthew 28:18–20).

Unauthorized Drivers

Do you remember what it was like to be young enough to live under the authority of others? When I was twelve and thirteen, I couldn't wait to grow up! I wanted the freedom of wheels. I wanted to be able to leave my house and go other places without my parents. Then after I turned sixteen and had my own set of wheels, I dreamed of the day I'd drive off to college and snip those apron strings just below the curfew and just above access to my mother's home cooking.

Remember what it was like to live under the authority of your parents? The most difficult year of my young life was 1978. I was fifteen with a learner's permit—licensed to sit behind the wheel of a car and travel the roads outside Atlanta, Georgia. Once I nearly killed my entire family learning to drive. I pulled across a dark highway, thinking the coast was clear, when an eighteen-wheeler blasted out of nowhere! My mother screamed, my sisters ducked, and my father prayed out loud. After our near miss, I was shaking like a leaf when I begged him to let me out of the driver's seat rather than have to continue the trip home. (He made me drive home.)

My father's favorite driving lessons were on the Sunday afternoon trips to my grandmas' houses. I would have enjoyed this had I been driving on country roads, but to get to our destinations I had to drive on interstates 75, 285, and 85 just to get around Atlanta. We often stopped at a rest area on the other side of the city traffic for me to stretch my legs and try to work the tension out of my neck. (I'm sure I was not the only one who was tense!)

All authority had not been given to me yet. I was still living under my father's tutelage and my mother's frazzled nerves. Although I never experienced what some call the "generation gap" many teenagers experience, when I was fifteen and learning to drive, I almost despised my parents. I had a hard time humbling myself to receive their constant, "Do this, do that, not now, but now, now, now!" And having now taught three fifteen-year-olds of my own to drive, I imagine they felt mostly the same about me.

> As you embrace the heart of God and the mind of Christ the power of God will be unleashed through you in both word and work.

Then, I passed my driver's test, and the state of Georgia licensed me to drive. I was authorized. With that authority, I drove to school, I drove to work, I drove to church, and I even carted my friends and sisters from here to there. Oh what freedom that authority brought!

Before Jesus appeared in Galilee, the people had only experienced teaching from those with learners permits. Just like me when I was learning to drive, the Pharisees often balked at the humility needed to interpret God's Word just right. The people suffered under poor teaching made almost unbearable by arrogant "unauthorized drivers" of the truth.

But when Jesus came, He taught as the One having authority. He did things no one else had done, and He said things no one else had said.

One day Jesus was teaching in the synagogue when an evil spirit cried out, "What do you want with us, Jesus of Nazareth? Have you come to destroy us? I know who you are—the Holy One of God!" (Mark 1:24).

Isn't that interesting? What men were slow to see, the demons declared immediately: "I know who you are—the Holy One of God!"

Rather than be frightened by the demon, rather than be confused as to what to say or do next, Jesus rebuked it: "Be quiet!" said Jesus sternly. "Come out of him!" (v. 25). And the demon had no choice but to obey because Jesus' position in heavenly order ranks far higher than the demons.

Once the demon left the man, the people were amazed. They were amazed because Jesus' words were full of authority and His actions backed them up. Read the entire story in Mark 1:23–28.

When the unauthorized met the authorized, they immediately recognized something different about Him: *What's this? Even the unclean spirits obey Him!* they thought.

Jesus spoke and acted with authority because He was the Son of God. Jesus was authorized. God allowed His supernatural power to be unleashed through Christ.

Perhaps people today don't pray because they have neglected the key to unlocking power in prayer. The power of God is not available to you if you do not share the heart of God. As you grow in your prayer life, as you embrace the heart of God and the mind of Christ—when the nature of Jesus becomes your priority—the power of God will be unleashed through you in both word and work.

Oh God, Please . . .

1. Begin to pray prayers that are powerful. Reflect on your salvation. Share how you came to know God personally.

2. Then ponder the cross. At the cross of Calvary, Jesus suffered and died, but in His death He won the victory over death! In His suffering He won the victory over sin! Share how you've personally experienced this victory in your own life.

3. Now, realize that in order to access the authority that Jesus expressed in His earthly ministry, you must embrace His complete surrender to His Father's will. What do you need to surrender to God?

Pray: I heard a friend pray this prayer. Will you join him?

Lord, I have a piece of paper here that represents my life. There are a whole lot of blanks that are not filled in. Nevertheless, I give it to You and trust You to take care of filling in the blanks. No matter where, no matter what, no matter with whom, I want to live my life in Jesus' name. Amen

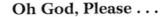

CHAPTER 11

Surrender Is Powerful

Jesus answered, "I am the way and the truth and the life. No one comes to the Father except through me. If you really knew me, you would know my Father as well. From now on, you do know him and have seen him."

— JOHN 14:6–7

J esus spoke and acted with authority on earth because He was the Son of God, and when Philip asked Jesus to just bring "the Father" to them, Jesus claimed that anyone who knew Him also knew His Father. Think about that for a minute, then read John 14:7–11.

Several years ago I helped lead a middle school girls retreat. We had planned to go to a lake house, but at the last minute torrential rain kept us closer to home (very much closer to home). On that Friday night twenty-eight middle school girls were camped out in my house for the weekend.

Prior to our retreat, several of the mothers had expressed their concern over their girls. These mothers shared the normal mother fears that accompany the dawning of the teen years. I knew these mothers well and wanted to reassure them that their girls were fine, but I didn't know the girls very well.

By Saturday morning, however, I was ready to truly tell those mothers they had nothing to worry about. As I sat in my den with those girls, I felt like I was sitting with their mothers. If I'd been blindfolded, I could have placed those girls with their mothers with nothing other than my ears. I knew their mothers, and therefore I knew those girls.

I cannot say that I want my daughters to be *just like* me, but I would like for them to resemble my better qualities. I cannot say that I want my son to be *just like* his father, but Tom has some characteristics that I pray T.J. will embrace. While earthly children resemble their parents, Jesus was the earthly Son of God who was *just like* His Father.

The Power of One

Often Jesus tells us that He and His Father are one. They are one mind, one heart, and one purpose and passion. They are in total and complete unity with each other.

Here we are again, talking about "oneness," but what does that have to do with power? If you have your Bible open as you read this book (and I hope that you do), read John 14:11–14. In particular, look at verses 13 and 14: "And I will do whatever you ask in my name, so that the Son may bring glory to the Father. You may ask me for anything in my name, and I will do it."

That sounds like a powerful promise to me, and as I think back over my own experience with Christ, I am frustrated by the many times I've cried and crumbled because I've not only felt powerless but also—is it OK to say this?—abandoned.

We all must embrace a critical truth if we want to experience power in our prayer lives: the secret to experiencing God's power flowing in and through our lives is absolute surrender and conscientious obedience to Him.

Jesus said, "The words that I say to you I do not speak on My own initiative, but the Father abiding in Me does His works" (John 14:10 NASB). When Jesus spoke, He spoke His Father's words, and they are accompanied by divine intervention and action. Note that in John 14:10 Jesus said that when

He spoke the Father's words the Father did His work.

Even Jesus said that His divine power and authority was made available through obedience and submission: "I tell you the truth, the Son

> The secret to experiencing God's power flowing in and through our lives is absolute surrender and conscientious obedience to Him.

can do nothing by himself; he can do only what he sees his Father doing, because whatever the Father does the Son also does. For the Father loves the Son and shows him all he does" (John 5:19–20a). And later in the same chapter, He said, "By myself I can do nothing; I judge only as I hear, and my judgment is just, for I seek not to please myself but him who sent me" (v. 30).

Note the key that unlocks access to God's authority and power is total surrender: "For I seek not to please myself but him who sent me." When you come to the place where you are completely surrendered to God's plan, to God's purpose, and to God's absolute authority in your life, then, and only then, are your prayers powerful.

Authorized Personnel Only

When my good husband Tom goes to the hospital to visit church members, he's often faced with a closed door and this sign: Authorized Personnel Only. When I see a door like that, I turn around and look for another way, or permission, to proceed. Not Tom. He marches right on through those doors with confidence that he earned his doctorate for such a time as this. If anyone asks about his credentials, he simply says, "I'm Dr.

Thomas McCoy, and I'm here to see _____." No one has ever sent him back from behind those closed doors.

Our daughter Kaleigh has always been a stickler for rules. Even when she was young, she couldn't tolerate even the slightest bending of the rules. When she heard her father did this, she said, "Daddy, you're not a *real* doctor! You're only a Bible doctor!" Tom's response was, "All the more reason for me to use my title to get me into forbidden places! What's more important, a person's body or their soul?"

When my daughter Mikel was growing up, we spent many summers watching her play softball. One summer my nieces were visiting us from Florida, and we took them with us to watch Mikel play ball in Crossville, Tennessee. I knew we'd be charged an entry fee, but when the gatekeeper told me I owed forty-eight dollars, I nearly had a fit. Imagine having to pay that much to watch your own daughter play ball! I mean, this is the child with whom I suffered five months of morning sickness and developed varicose veins to bring into this world! This is the girl I carted to rec league games two, sometimes three times a week for six years! Who did her laundry and fed her meals so that she'd be able to show up at that park to play?! . . . I paid the forty-eight bucks and watched the game.

I've already mentioned to you that I went to India several years ago on a mission trip. To get into the country, though, I had to purchase a tourist visa. While it would be good for ten years, it was expensive and the Indian government had to grant it to me. I had to complete the application and place my request before at least one official could declare, "OK," to opening India's borders and letting me come through. They had all the say, and without a visa, I would not go in.

I tell these stories to remind you of what it is like to be granted authority to go into a place otherwise closed to you. Jesus said, "He *who believes in Me*, the works that I do, he will do also; and greater works than these he will do; because I go to the Father. Whatever you ask *in My name*, that will I do, so that the Father may be glorified in the Son. If you ask Me anything *in My name*, I will do it" (John 14:12–14 NASB, italics added).

In these verses Jesus gave us a bold promise. He opened wide a door posted with the sign Authorized Personnel Only. Only those who believe in Him and ask in His name are granted entry.

Although God created you—even knit you together in your mother's womb—He still chose to pay the outrageous price of your redemption and let His very own Son suffer and die in your place so that you could enter this place of authority. The cross does not even begin to compare to the forty-eight dollars I spent to watch Mikel play ball.

> When we approach the throne of grace we come with authority because of who we know.

And when we come to God, we must realize that entry depends entirely on Him. He gave us the application (Romans 10:9–10), and when we complete it to His satisfaction, He assures us His "borders" are open to us. Jesus said, "I am the way and the truth and the life. No one comes to the Father except through me" (John 14:6). Now we march boldly through the door marked for only the authorized; and when confronted with our right to be there, we see our Savior Jesus Christ sitting at our Father's right hand, and we boldly proclaim, "I come in Jesus' name!"

Oh God, Please . . .

Perhaps we should begin our prayers with "in Jesus' name" rather than end them there. That way we could be reminded that when we approach the throne of grace we come with authority because of who we know. You've heard of having friends in "high places." Well, that is exactly the kind of friend we have in Jesus—only He's the Friend in the highest place.

1. Share an experience you've had when you were given permission to go somewhere that was otherwise off limits to you.

2. How does Jesus' authority and your relationship with Him impact your prayers?

Pray: When you pray today, close your eyes and visualize that door marked with the sign Authorized Personnel Only. Imagine pushing through that door and marching boldly up to God's throne of grace. Sit with Him there, and listen to His voice. Ask Him what He'd have you do today that will allow the world to know Him.

Father, thank You for allowing me to be right here—in Your presence, able to talk without interruption and with no reservations. Thank You for being approachable. I am humbled that You allow me to come. Jesus, thank You. Because I know that You love me, and that You hear me when I pray, . . . [continue your prayer]. Amen

CHAPTER 12

In Harmony with Jesus

"I am the vine; you are the branches. If a man remains in me and I in him, he will bear much fruit; apart from me you can do nothing."

— JOHN 15:5

When we pray in Jesus' name, we are praying in harmony with Jesus. Don't forget that thinking God's thoughts, obeying God's instructions, and choosing to love what God loves is the secret to accessing the power of God. To experience power in prayer, you must understand the concept of living in harmony with (or in oneness with) God. Jesus explained this concept with a grapevine.

> *"I am the true vine, and my Father is the gardener. He cuts off every branch in me that bears no fruit, while every branch that does bear fruit he prunes so that it will be even more fruitful. You are already clean because of the word I have spoken to you. Remain in me, and I will remain in you. No branch can bear fruit by itself; it must remain in the vine. Neither can you bear fruit unless you remain in me.*
>
> *"I am the vine; you are the branches. If a man remains in me and I in him, he will bear much fruit; apart from me you can do nothing. If anyone does not remain in me, he is like a branch that is thrown away and withers; such branches are picked up, thrown*

into the fire and burned. If you remain in me and my words remain in you, ask whatever you wish, and it will be given you. This is to my Father's glory, that you bear much fruit, showing yourselves to be my disciples." (John 15:4–8)

Can a branch bear fruit by itself? No, not at all. In fact any branch that finds itself separated from the vine might look alive but is certainly dead. Branches that are cut off of the vine will wither and die.

What happens if we remain in Christ? We bear fruit. Our prayers will be powerful and effective; our teaching will be delivered with authority; and our ministry will be illustrated by supernatural power. But to experience powerful prayer and to live like genuine disciples of Christ—to bear fruit—how.does "remaining in Jesus" practically break down?

- ➤ Read His Word.
- ➤ Apply His teaching to life.
- ➤ Deny any desire that is contrary to God's Word.

Jesus is the vine; we are the branches. We can do absolutely nothing apart from Christ. The branches that refuse the vine will be thrown away. They are eventually burned.

The Gardener

The branches the gardener removes meet the same end. Let's talk about those branches for a moment. According to John 15:1–8, there are two ways to separate from the vine. One is to be cut off by the careful pruning of the Master Gardener, and the other is to cut yourself off because you don't want to be connected.

What happens when the Gardener does the cutting? Let me see if I can explain. In our lives we experience times of severe disappointment. Your disappointment and mine are most likely different, but we share the same grief, confusion, frustration, and general sense of being "undone" when these things happen.

If we are not careful we may cut ourselves off from the vine by insisting that the Gardener put those branches back where they were. We can pitch such a fit over the "wounds" His pruning created that we might find ourselves in a heap of despair on top of withering branches.

I've been pruned a time or two, and I've often pitched a fit. That's something we do here in the south where I grew up, and I've learned a thing or two about fit pitching. When the Gardener is at work, I need to yield to His expertise. When He is cutting is not the time for me to try to impress Him with my branch-growing skills. He has never yet stopped His pruning on me because I cried out in pain. He lets me cry and continues His cutting.

And if I decide that what He has removed is too painful for me to bear, and if I choose to doubt Him, then I will

> The ultimate goal of answered prayer is the glory of God.

lose the fellowship and camaraderie and oneness I have with Him. For a time I will be OK—maybe even still producing one last grape that was already ripening before the branch was removed. Eventually, however, I will begin to wither. I'll lose the joy of my salvation; I will sense that God and I are no longer close, and I will lose the power I have to "overcome the things of this world."

When the Gardener is cutting, I need to focus on Him, not on what He's doing. I need to remember He loves me and trust that, in time, the wounds that are necessary will heal in such a way that I will certainly bear more fruit than imaginable.

This difficult truth is followed by another tremendous promise: "If you remain in me and my words remain in you, ask whatever you wish, and it will be given you" (John 15:7). What is the prerequisite to receiving "whatever you wish"? Remain in Christ and let His words remain you.

Don't forget that the ultimate goal of answered prayer is the glory of God. According to John 15:8 our fruit production is directly linked not only to our remaining in Christ but also to the glory of the Father being revealed in and through us.

Reflect

The John 15 verses illustrate the principle of praying in harmony, or in "oneness," with Jesus. Remember the WWJD bracelets? When we pray in Jesus' name, we in essence say, "This prayer is in keeping with what Jesus would do if He were here." Before we present our requests to God, perhaps we would do well to ask ourselves, "What would Jesus do?"

> Prayer is about me laying down my agenda, never to pick it up again.

Internationally known British theologian Selwyn Hughes said, "Prayer is cooperation with God. In prayer you align your will, your desires, your life to God." He goes on to say, "Prayer is surrender—the surrendering of *all* we are in order to receive *all* that is an offer from the divine hands."

This reminds me of what I've been reading when I see phrases such as "*whatever* you ask in My name," "*anything* you ask in My name," "*whatever* you wish . . . it will be given you." *Whatever* and *anything* sound like all to me!

Prayer is about me laying down my agenda, never to pick it up again. Still, in prayer I'm not left empty. I pour myself out in surrender to be filled to all fullness in power. That is the mystery Jesus was explaining in John 15. When we pray in harmony with Jesus, we have *whatever we wish!*

Let me borrow more profound words from Selwyn Hughes:

> We continue looking at prayer as surrender—a surrender of our purposes, plans, will, and desires into the hands of God. But . . . surrender does not imply weak negativism. Prayer is like the wire that surrenders to the dynamo, the flower to the sun, the student to the teacher. *The Gulf Stream will flow through a drinking straw, provided the straw is aligned to the Gulf Stream and is not blocked in any way. You, as an individual, surrender to God in prayer, and then God gives Himself to you.* . . . There is a thrilling verse in Revelation 3:21 that says, "To him who overcomes, I will give the right to sit down with My Father on His throne." Ever thought about that? Here is the Christ, the Son of God, telling poor mortals that just as He sat down with His Father on the throne, so we are to sit with Him on the throne. Of course, this verse is referring to something that is yet to happen, but in one sense it

happens right now. When we surrender
to Him and cooperate with Him, then we
share the ideas and powers which rule the
universe. We share His throne! We are
part of the ruling ideas and powers which
guide and govern the universe. [1]

That is an amazing thought. When I turn loose of my
dreams, my ambition, my desires, and my plans, I open myself wide to receive in return the dreams, ambitions, desires,
and plans of the Creator of the universe, the God of glory! It's
like trading my baby doll Santa brought at Christmas when I
was eight for my live and kicking baby daughter when I was
twenty-eight! I'll take God's plans over my own any day!

Prayer that Jesus Sanctions

When we pray in Jesus' name, we are going directly to the
Father and boldly asking for Him to respond. "In that day you
will no longer ask me anything. I tell you the truth, my Father
will give you whatever you ask in my name" (John 16:23). Jesus promised that His death so completely paved the way for
our access to His Father that we can go directly to God! He
told us that when we pray our petitions hold the same "umph"
that His held when He prayed from earth.

But at the risk of sounding redundant, let me remind you
that this kind of praying is the kind that mirrors Jesus in Gethsemane before His arrest: "Not my will, but yours be done"
(Luke 22:42).

Don't be alarmed if you discover that this kind of praying
takes more time and effort. It's easy to take my shopping list
to the local grocery and fill the cart with what I think I want.

It's much more difficult to evaluate my eating habits ahead of time, choose to set goals to eat more fresh fruit and vegetables, and then purchase only what I need to fulfill those plans. That kind of shopping takes discipline, desire, and denial of my flesh.

In order to pray the kind of prayers that Jesus guarantees God will answer, you will have to come to your prayer closet more willing to listen than to talk. When you pray, meditate on God's Word and reflect on His goodness. Take whatever time (and energy) it takes to go through the painful process of killing (crucifying) the self who rises against God. Yield to His authority in your life. Do the hard work of developing discipline to embrace God's desire and deny your own (when your desires are contrary to God's). Learn to take no for an answer.

> His death so completely paved the way for our access to His Father that we can go directly to God!

Is God anxious to hear about our plans? Is it He who anticipates checking in with us so we can set His agenda? God is not like Santa Claus! Santa sets his elves in motion in response to the long list of wishes he receives from the good little boys and girls. (Our society weaves many subtle deceptions into our doctrine of prayer that find their roots in our American culture of Santa Claus—a works-based theology and a god who delivers wishes, to name a few. We will discuss this further in the next chapter.)

Watchman Nee says this about prayer sanctioned by Jesus:

> Over the same matter there is the possibility of having two different kinds of prayer. One kind has its source in our

own will. It is based on our own thinking and our own expectations. The Lord may hear and answer our prayer, but such prayer has a very low value attached to it. If, on the other hand, we bring this matter before God and let His Spirit merge our will into God's will and our thought into God's thought, we shall discover within us a deep longing which is in fact a reproduction of His will and thought . . . prayer which is prayed according to His will has worth and weight . . . how precious and substantial is prayer such as this. It can hallow God's name, bring in God's kingdom, and cause God's will to prevail on earth as in heaven.[2]

Oh God, Please . . .

Praying in the name of Jesus means praying in harmony with Him. Think about the things you and He have talked about these past few months. Is there any will of your own still seeping into your requests? If so, ask God to give you supernatural power to let go of whatever you're holding.

Think about the drinking straw illustration. Consider the power of the Gulf Stream. When I first wrote the following words, Hurricane Wilma was moving northwest at 7 mph between Cuba and Central America, headed toward the Yucatan Peninsula. It was a Wednesday, and hurricane preparations were already underway in southern Florida (which was northeast of Wilma's path). Why were Floridians preparing for Wilma? Because the Jet Stream (another powerful force in the atmosphere) was pressing south and had the power to take history's strongest recorded hurricane (with winds reaching 175 mph on the day I was writing) and change its course. Predictions were that Wilma would make landfall on the western coast of Florida Sunday morning (moving northeast rather than continuing in its northwest path). That is a powerful gust of wind!

You are like the drinking straw, and God is like the Gulf Stream; when you bow before Him in prayer, however, He is like the Jet Stream. The Power of the universe desires to have fellowship with you, and He's promised to allow His power to flow in and through you when you line yourself up with Him.

I'm not sure our tiny little minds can even begin to comprehend what might happen if our church were to line herself up corporately with God's ambitions, desires, and plans. If we prayed in harmony with Jesus, we could move mountains of doubt, shift the course of hurricanes of destruction, and experience spiritual earthquakes of awakening.

1. What would you like to see God do in your church?

2. If God's power were to flow through you, what might happen in your family? Among your friends? In your workplace?

3. What do you find most difficult about lining your will up with God's?

Pray: *Lord, I recognize that You alone are power. I long to experience Your power flowing in and through me. Show me where I am harboring ambitions and desires that are in contrast to Your goals for Your kingdom. As You show me specific areas of my life that need to be yielded to You, I will yield those areas of my life to You. Even if it is difficult to do so, Lord, I'm asking that You take out of me whatever needs to be taken out so that You can put in me everything that You want to put in. I trust You, Lord. In Jesus' powerful name I pray. Amen*

CHAPTER 13

Santa, Petitions, and Prayer

When you ask, you do not receive, because you ask with wrong motives, that you may spend what you get on your pleasures.

— JAMES 4:3

How have you subconsciously treated God like Santa Claus? I'm not anti-Santa; I love the jolly ol' elf! But it is just like Satan to turn our attention from Jesus at such a holy time of the year and focus it instead on a character who directly opposes two critical elements of God's nature: His holiness and His righteousness.

God's Holiness

"Santa's making a list, checking it twice, gonna find out who's naughty and nice . . ." You've seen the pictures of the white-bearded man sitting in his rocking chair, bifocals perched on his nose, carefully checking off his long list. And if you dig deep in the recesses of your psyche, you might discover that you have another image there in the shadows. You may think that God is in the list-making business. Do you have "the Man upstairs" propped back in His La-Z-Boy with a long list in His hands? Is He cursing all the bad people and blessing all the good ones? Where are you on that list?

> The holiness of God doesn't make a list; He doesn't need to.

When I was journeying through the prayer experience that infertility offered me years ago, God exposed my own list-making theology. When I got painfully honest with God, I cried at the injustice of my infertility as it stood face-to-face with the fertility of women who have abortions. God quickly reminded me that none of my petitions have any merit based on my righteousness.

The holiness of God doesn't make a list; He doesn't need to. One sin and we're done for! God doesn't have to take the time to list them. I've heard it explained that if I were making an omelet and used six good eggs and cracked a seventh but found it rotten and used it anyway, my omelet would be ruined.

> Come to God in the humble knowledge that nothing separates you from those "less deserving."

One bad egg ruins an omelet just as one sin ruins any hope of my own righteousness somehow making a stand for itself in the presence of a holy God. That truth is perhaps the number-one lie embraced by millions of Americans. Somehow most people believe that, in the end, if the good outweighs the bad they'll get to go to heaven. Nothing could be further from the truth.

Santa might take the time to check his list. Santa might weigh the good against the bad, but Santa is not God. We all know this by now, but I'll still state the reminder that Santa isn't even real!

God has a few books, not a list. A list of names is in one of His books, and a recording of deeds is in the other. The book of names is called the Lamb's Book of Life, and only those who have accepted Jesus as Lord and Savior have their names recorded there. The only people who will go to heaven when they die are those whose names are recorded in the Lamb's

Book of Life. (Read Revelation 20:11–15 for a glimpse of a day when we will all be gathered in one place and witness the reading of God's books.)

When you pray, don't wave your good works in the face of God like a badge that ought to get you into the chamber of blessings. Come to God in the humble knowledge that nothing separates you from those "less deserving." Cast yourself on His amazing grace and infinite mercy.

God's Righteousness

Every year children live in expectation of Santa's elves working hard to make the toys that will fulfill their dreams. Then, almost without any serious thought, these children grow into adults and believe God is "up there" to give them what they want. God often gives us what we want, but He also withholds His blessings in order to open our eyes to what we really need. God lends His supernatural power to fulfilling His own plans because He knows that what He wants for us far outweighs what we could ever think to ask for!

The righteousness of God remains determined to stay on course with His purpose until the end of time. He will not be manipulated by the whims of men and women who pray selfish prayers for selfish purposes. James tried to explain this to us: "You do not have, because you do not ask God. When you ask, you do not receive, because you ask with wrong motives, that you may spend what you get on your pleasures" (James 4:2–3).

What You Ask Reveals Much about You

Turn in your Bible to 1 Kings 3:1–15. In verse 5 God said to Solomon, "Ask for whatever you want me to give you."

This Old Testament account of Solomon's response to God's offer provides us a great illustration of what it means to pray in Jesus' name. God offered Solomon "whatever," and Solomon responded with integrity and selflessness. Solomon's only request was for God to give him a discerning heart so that he could govern God's people fairly (see v. 9).

Because God was pleased that Solomon asked for this, He gave him what he asked for and added to it. "Since you have asked for this and not for long life or wealth for yourself, nor have asked for the death of your enemies but for discernment in administering justice, I will do what you have asked. I will give you a wise and discerning heart, so that there will never have been anyone like you, nor will there ever be. Moreover, I will give you what you have not asked for—both riches and honor—so that in your lifetime you will have no equal among kings. And if you walk in my ways and obey my statutes and commands as David your father did, I will give you a long life" (1 Kings 3:11–14).

> When God invites you to come to Him in prayer, He is eager to pour His blessing into your life.

What you ask for reveals much about you. When God invites you to come to Him in prayer, He is eager to pour His blessing into your life. But when you come to pray, you need to be careful that you ask for what will honor Him most.

Ben Patterson writes, "The way you respond to an unlimited offer will say a lot about who you are inside. God says, 'You can have anything you want, go ahead and ask, and it shall be yours, and [then he] adds, implicitly, 'and what you ask will reveal you.' Is that why Jesus said, 'You may ask me for anything in my name, and I will do it' (John 14:14)? The sky's the limit—if you ask in his name. But what you ask will reveal what you know about his name, how congruent your heart is with the heart of God. Your desires say much about you."[3]

When my children, Mikel, Kaleigh, and T.J., were still in diapers (all three of them at the same time, yipes!), I was committed to a daily jog of anywhere between three and five miles. My jogging time was my alone time, so the amount I needed (and the time Tom had to give me) dictated the distance I jogged. It also was an extension of my quiet time. I read my Bible then laced up my Nikes and took off down the driveway with the Scripture still marinating in my head. God and I visited—just the two of us—for the next thirty to forty-five minutes (the only minutes in the course of the day when I didn't have little people clamoring for my attention). On one of these mornings I was jogging down Buckner Road about a mile and a half from home. Right in front of Churchill Estates I distinctly heard God's voice ask this question: "Leighann, what do you want?"

Have you ever heard God speak in such a way that you *knew* there was much more to be heard than merely His words? This was just such a time. The question caught me off guard, and I wasn't sure how to respond. I sensed that God was seriously offering me *whatever* I wanted! My answer had to be different than, "Tell me where to go to college; give me a husband; help me with this paper; I need a job; oh, I want a baby . . ."—the endless list of requests I'd already sent heavenward. This time God was offering me a blank check and asking me to fill it in.

I responded, "Oh, Lord, I don't know. I mean You've given me so much already—a husband who loves me, a great house, three beautiful children, and my health. What more could I want?" But I knew that answering God's offer with a question wasn't really answering Him at all. I finished my jog, got busy with my preschoolers, and didn't think much more about it.

Then, a few weeks later I woke up in the middle of the night and heard God's voice again, "Leighann, I want to give you whatever you ask for. This is your chance! What do you want?"

This time I sat up in bed and wondered at His intent. Why was God asking me this? Didn't I already tell Him what I wanted (all the time!)? "I want sleep! Help T.J. sleep through the night! Give me time to write (I wrote curriculum units for children's Sunday school during these days and lived under the pressure of deadlines), and please let Walmart have the diapers in stock." But I knew deep in my heart that God was looking for an answer much deeper than that. I honestly didn't know how to respond, so I turned over and went back to sleep.

> When I came to that place of complete surrender, peace and joy flooded my soul.

A few days later I was working at my computer and, again, God said, "Leighann, what do you want?" By now I was concerned that I hadn't answered both times He'd asked me before. I struggled to come up with something. Sure I had dreams of writing and being published, of a future teaching ministry, and I so wanted our church to grow large (I'd never been a part of a small church before, except for the few months I spent at B. H. Carroll Baptist Church in Ft. Worth, Texas, where I went solely for the purpose of snagging Tom McCoy). But none of these dreams seemed worthy of a blank check. They all seemed to somehow come up short in the face of an unlimited offer.

Finally, after struggling to find *something* to ask of God, I answered, "Lord! What do You want me to want?!"

And to that He responded, "Exactly!"

God wanted me to yield myself completely to Him. He wanted me to trust Him with my dreams, my plans, and my future. And when I came to that place of complete surrender, peace and joy flooded my soul. This happened many years ago, but as I write about it now that peace washes over me again.

Oh God, Please . . .

In that devotion Ben Patterson wrote relating to Solomon in 1 Kings 3, he went on to say, "The enemy of God's best is not the worst, but the less than the best, the good things."

Are you willing to stop clinging to the good things and hold out for God's best? If so, tell Him. Patterson also said, "God's complaint is that we want too little, not too much."

C. S. Lewis said, "We are half-hearted creatures, fooling about with drink and sex and ambition when infinite joy is offered us, like an ignorant child who wants to go on making mud pies in a slum because he cannot imagine what is meant by the offer of a holiday at the sea. We are far too easily pleased."

1. Do your prayers reflect the vast riches you have in Christ?

2. What you ask reveals much about you. How would you answer if God were to say, "Ask for whatever you want Me to give you"?

Pray: *Father, thank You for offering me exceedingly, abundantly more than I could ever ask or even imagine. I want to let You give me whatever You see fit. I want You to be glorified in my life and in the lives of my husband and children. I want to live each day aware of Your goodness, Your love, and Your power. I want others to see Jesus in me.*

PART 4

In Jesus' Name I Pray, Amen

Prayer is not overcoming God's reluctance,
but laying hold of His willingness.

—

MARTIN LUTHER

CHAPTER 14

Praying in the Name of Jesus

"Therefore God exalted him to the highest place and gave him the name that is above every name, that at the name of Jesus every knee should bow, in heaven and on earth and under the earth, and every tongue confess that Jesus Christ is Lord, to the glory of God the Father."

— PHILIPPIANS 2:9–11

Kids and Prayer

Three-year-old Reese:
*"Our Father, Who does art in heaven,
Harold is His name. Amen."*

_____

A little boy was overheard praying:
*"Lord, if you can't make me a better boy, don't worry about it.
I'm having a real good time like I am."*

_____

I had been teaching my three-year old daughter,
Caitlin, the Lord's Prayer.
For several evenings at bedtime, she would repeat after me
the lines from the prayer. Finally, she decided to go solo.
I listened with pride as she carefully enunciated
each word right up to the end of the prayer.

"Lead us not into temptation," she prayed,
"but deliver us some E-mail. Amen."

And one particular four-year-old prayed:
*"And forgive us our trash baskets
as we forgive those who put trash in our baskets."*

A wife invited some people to dinner.
At the table, she turned to her six-year-old daughter and
asked, "Would you like to say the blessing?"
"I wouldn't know what to say," the girl replied.
"Just say what you hear Mommy say," the wife answered.
The daughter bowed her head and said,
"Lord, why on earth did I invite all these people to dinner?"

Isn't it funny how children put thoughts together? I wonder
whether God and Jesus chuckle as They peer over heaven's edge and listen to our prayers. I wonder whether God
laughs out loud when we get all mixed up. I like to think that
He does.

But I'm not sure that praying amiss is always such a laughing matter. James 4:3 says, "You ask and don't receive because
you ask wrongly" (HCSB).

Praying for the wrong things and praying in the wrong
way are actually not funny at all. Jesus gave us some powerful
promises in John regarding praying in His name. Many people
have taken these words out of context and waved them about
like some kind of purchase order as a guarantee that God is
somehow obligated to answer their prayers. They've used these

promises to secure success on earth—proclaiming that if we all just ask in Jesus' name we will impact heaven with earth's pleasure rather than penetrate earth with heaven's glory.

If we distort the application of these promises, we are pitiful at best and devastated at worst. We absolutely must understand exactly what Jesus was promising and then respond in humility.

Read (and underline) these verses in your copy of God's Word: John 14:13–14; 15:16; and 16:23–24, 26–27. (See appendix, "Scriptural Basis for Praying in Jesus' Name.")

Jesus taught us to present our requests to God in Jesus' name, so we ask in Jesus' name. Is this a formula for instant success? Does "in Jesus name, amen" stamp our requests and send them on their way? Do we actually receive *everything* and *anything* we ever ask for in the name of Jesus? Is God's Word ever *not* true? If God's Word is always true and if we even once or twice pray in Jesus' name and fail to receive what we're asking, how can this be?

I'm going to answer these questions in this chapter and the following chapters and tell you how I know that prayer is powerful.

It's More than a Name

To begin, I want you to understand what a name represented in the Bible. Proverbs 22:1a says this: "A good name is to be chosen rather than great riches" (NKJV). Ecclesiastes 7:1a says, "A good name is better than precious ointment" (NKJV).

In biblical times names were much more than a way to identify one person from the other. Names represented character, purpose, and destiny. The origin of our last names are similar to this. My mother's maiden name is "Smith." Most likely her European ancestors were blacksmiths, silversmiths, or—I like to think—goldsmiths. Our surnames are linked to our heritage.

The Bible includes instances when God changed people's names as they grew in their relationship with Him. He used these name changes to communicate

> *A good name is to be chosen rather than great riches.*
>
> PROVERBS 22:1A NKJV

their place in His plan. Abram (exalted father) became Abraham (father of many), and Sarai (princess) became Sarah (princess with authority to rule). Jacob (he deceives) became Israel (he struggles with God), and Simon (he has heard) became Peter (rock).

The name of Jesus means "The Lord is Salvation," which carries with it His character, His purpose, and His destiny. Jesus' character is love. His purpose is to demonstrate God's love. His destiny is oneness with God and eternal life.

When we pray in Jesus' name, we are praying inside the boundaries of His character. When we pray in Jesus' name, we are praying according to His purpose. And when we pray in Jesus' name, we are praying toward the destiny He's already secured (complete unity with God and eternal life in His presence)—the same one we have yet to grasp.

These next three chapters will summarize the previous ones. Prayer is powerful when we pray in Jesus' name. Praying in Jesus' name means to pray:

- by the authority of Jesus;
- in harmony with Jesus; and
- prayers that are sanctioned by Jesus.

Let's revisit each of these one at a time.

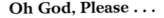

Oh God, Please . . .

1. Consider the things you want God to do for you. Do those requests fit inside the parameters of Jesus' character? His purpose? His destiny?

2. How might your requests change?

3. Can you think of Bible verses that apply to your requests? If so, share them.

When you pray, invite God to give you His perspective on your requests so that your heart and His come into unity with each other. Expand your requests to reflect Jesus' character, purpose, and destiny.

Pray: *Lord, give me Your perspective on my requests. Tell me how Your ways are higher than mine, and reassure me that You know what You're doing. I have such a hard time seeing things the way You see them. You are eternal, and I'm still caught in this finite life on earth. You are wise, and my wisdom is foolishness to You. You control Your emotions, and mine sometimes control me. Oh God, please give me Your perspective so that I can nestle in close to Your heart and willingly wait on what You are doing. Amen*

CHAPTER 15

Praying by the Authority of Jesus (Revisited)

Because you are sons, God sent the Spirit of his Son into our hearts, the Spirit who calls out, "Abba, Father."

— GALATIANS 4:6

After several years of being a pastor's wife, I met a woman I did not like. The feeling was mutual, and rather than deal with it personally or privately she caused me lots of grief by talking to others about me (and Tom). Eventually conversations drifted toward challenging my call to ministry and my "right" to serve so freely at our church.

Let me take a minute here to explain how tradition has defined the role of a pastor's wife in my denomination. Traditionally, pastor's wives played the piano, taught children's Sunday school classes, and fed visiting preachers delicious Sunday dinners. Over the years her role expanded to include leading women's ministries—perhaps teaching a ladies class on Sunday mornings and maybe even organizing events that raised awareness of missions and/or ministered to people "less fortunate than we."

Pastor's wives didn't coordinate the educational ministry of the church. They didn't recruit volunteers to serve across the board in the various ministries of the church, and they certainly didn't lead task forces to write the church's constitution and by-laws. But I felt called and equipped to do exactly these things.

Tom and I came to Thompson's Station when we were twenty-five years old right out of seminary. We joined eight regular attenders and were given the charge, "Please, lead us to become a church." My spiritual gifts include administration and leadership. Because it was just us, Tom and I rolled up our sleeves and worked arm in arm to do what we could to join God in growing our congregation into a church. After seven years we had well more than two hundred people in attendance and a full program, and we were constituted into a church (complete with by-laws and a policy and procedures manual). I had been an integral part in all of these things.

What started as a personality conflict was fueled by spiritual warfare and became dissension in the body. Soon groups of people began to challenge my "position" and asked (not so much in their words but by subtle hints), "By whose authority are you doing these things?"

> When God gives us visions
> He uses our history,
> our memories, and our
> emotions attached to them.

I had already been working outside the imaginary lines that drew traditional boundaries around the pastors' wife and had enjoyed the freedom of "drawing outside the lines." Inside, however, I struggled with the tradition I'd been reared in and the creative liberties Tom and I were taking. So when others began to speak aloud the same words that I fought in my mind, it was almost too much.

As much as partnering with Tom in ministry was like a dream come true, I found myself begging God to release me from my call. I did not like being the recipient of such harsh criticism, and I certainly didn't want to be the cause of disunity in our church. Mostly whining and asking God to release me from my service at this church, one day I was crying out to Him and said, "They don't want me, so let me go!" . . . And God gave me a vision.

The Family of God

Now, before you discredit me because I just told you that God "gave me a vision," let me assure you that I rarely ever have these. While I'm not afraid of visions, I'm just not accustomed to them and have had only two in my lifetime. Most often God speaks to me through His Word. Sometimes, however, when my struggles are deep, He uses my own creative energy and communicates to me through my imagination. This particular vision came to me while I was awake. I was sitting at my computer trying to meet one of my curriculum writing deadlines, and I couldn't shake the struggle with the conflict we were suffering in our church. (My other vision came to me while I was sleeping. I am sure I'll write all about that one in a book someday.)

In my vision I was playing in a pile of dirt with a few other children. We were in front of an old Southern plantation home, enjoying the shade provided by great big oaks that lined the drive leading to the house. It was like a scene from *Gone with the Wind*.

I think that when God gives us visions He uses our history, our memories, and our emotions attached to them. My vision came out of my childhood memories. No, unfortunately, I didn't grow up on a lovely plantation (most of the lovely plantation homes that once stood where I grew up were burned on General Sherman's march to the sea), but I did take a field trip to the Fox Theater in Atlanta, Georgia, to watch *Gone with the Wind* when I was in the eighth grade. Most of us Southern girls are pretty certain we would have lived on plantations had we lived during the second half of the nineteenth century.

Back to my vision. I felt content in my dirt pile and was actually having fun even though one of the friends who was playing in the dirt with me was the woman I mentioned earlier. We were getting along OK as we interacted with the other children (they were slaves).

In the middle of this peaceful scene, a servant came out of the house and called to me from the porch. "Leighann, your Father wants to see you!"

Immediately his words caused fear to rise from deep inside me. My Father was a serious man. He was proud and righteous. He wasn't given to childish games, He didn't laugh much, and He had absolutely *no* tolerance for misbehavior. Don't get me wrong. He was also good, and I knew He loved me very much. But being summoned to Him immediately filled my heart with dread. Reluctantly and with much trembling, I followed the servant into the house.

My vision was so real I could smell the mahogany on the large front door, the tobacco in a pipe somewhere nearby, and the wood in the fire. I hung back in the grand foyer for a minute; I didn't really want to go in to where my Father was. Still, I knew that when my Father called, the only way to respond was with obedience.

I heard the crackling of the fire and paused to notice the glow it sent across the room where my Father sat. As soon as I walked through the entrance of the study, my heart immediately relaxed. Sitting on the hearth right in front of that fire was my big Brother! He and I knew each other quite well. We spent lots of time together. He tossed me in the air and caught me just in time. He let me ride with Him on His horse, and we'd chase rabbits through the fields. I could tell Him anything and knew He understood without judging me. When I was with Him, nothing else mattered.

Not only that, but my Brother also had an incredible relationship with our Father. When He was not with me, He was always with our Father. They spent days together discussing the family business. My Father loved my older Brother, and I

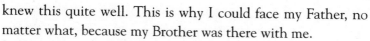

knew this quite well. This is why I could face my Father, no matter what, because my Brother was there with me.

This is where my vision ended.

Obedience above All

Speaking more to my spirit than to my mind, my vision was so powerful that it somewhat scared me. What should I take away from this? What was God trying to teach me? . . . A reminder for all of us: when we are uncertain whether an experience is truly a word from the Lord, a good way to pray is *"Father, if this is from You, please confirm it in Your Word."*

When I said that prayer, God sent me to Galatians 4. He didn't audibly say, "Leighann, go to Galatians 4." Instead, He caused me to remember that He spoke a few times in the Bible about the relationship we have with Him as children to their father and with Christ as siblings. So, I looked in my concordance for words such as *children*, *Abba*, and *slaves*. I knew about the Romans 8 passage and the Ephesians 1 reference to us being joint heirs with Christ, but on the day of my vision I was not as familiar with Galatians 4.

I do hope you are still keeping your Bible close as you read this book. Stop long enough to read Galatians 4:1–9.

I cannot tell you how excited I was to read the first five words of Galatians 4:1. Remember that I asked God to confirm my vision in His Word? The first five words of Galatians 4:1 say this, "What I am saying is."

In the next nine verses God gave me the meaning of my dream. Let me share it

> A good way to pray is *"Father, if this is from You, please confirm it in Your Word."*

with you so that you can understand a bit more about how God speaks to us through visions and so that you can understand what it means to pray in the authority of Jesus.

Fully, Galatians 4:1 says, "What I am saying is that as long as the heir is a child, he is no different from a slave, although he owns the whole estate." Continue reading through verse 3.

When I was in the dirt pile, I was playing with the slave children; I was like them! Well, really I wasn't, but I thought I was. The funny thing was that I didn't mind being the same as them and I kind of liked not being different.

Reread verses 4–7, and especially focus on verse 7: "So you are no longer a slave, but a son; and since you are a son, God has made you also an heir."

When the servant called me to my Father, God reminded me I was born a daughter of the King. At eleven years old, I'd received His gift of salvation while attending camp in the north Georgia mountains. When I was fifteen I responded to God's call to full-time vocational Christian service as a result of participating in my first mission trip to upper state New York. I nailed that call down while sitting beside railroad tracks watching the sun set somewhere in Nevada as a summer missionary at age twenty-one. And the people who had challenged my "authority" to serve God at Thompson's Station Church were unable to take that call away.

In my dream I *knew* I was a child of the Owner of that plantation. I knew I wasn't a slave child, nor was I a visitor; I *knew* I belonged to Him. This was Galatians 4:6 shouting in my ears: *"Because you are [daughters], God sent the Spirit of his Son into our hearts, the Spirit who calls out, 'Abba, Father.'"*

God reminded me in His Word that as an heir I had work to do. I couldn't worry about what the others were saying; I couldn't stay in the yard playing—I had to be about the work God called me to.

He actually "spanked" me with verse 9: "But now that you know God—or rather are known by God—how is it that you are turning back to those weak and miserable principles? Do you wish to be enslaved by them all over again?" With a gentle, loving, firm, and powerful reminder, God said to me, "I called you, I prepared you, I brought you—how is it now that you are listening to these voices of defeat and turning to the weak and worthless things of this world?"

But mostly, through this vision the Holy Spirit penetrated my heart with the truth of the authority that is mine in Jesus' name. I can't adequately describe how relieved, comforted, understood, and satisfied I felt when I saw Jesus in that room! Because of Him, I could get out of the dirt and receive whatever command my Father had for me.

When we pray in Jesus' name, we enter into personal audience with God. We come into the presence of God with the same authority that Jesus has with Him. We come with a call on our lives—with purpose and destiny that are extensions of the purpose and destiny God had for Jesus when He walked among us.

If you have already responded to God's "call" on your life—if you have accepted Jesus as your Savior, and you anticipate going to heaven when you die—then you have received Him as Lord of your life. And if He is Lord, then you can be certain that He has work for you to do.

What are you doing in the dirt piles of this world when God has bigger, better, greater plans for your life? It's time to get up, get busy, and take hold of your God-given responsibility with confidence and compassion because you are clothed with the authority of Jesus' name.

Oh God, Please . . .

If you'd rather play in the dirt with the slaves, you can pray but your prayers will fall far short of God's plans and purposes for you. Because you are willing to make mud pies when God called you to change the world, your prayers will never have power.

But if you'll respond to the call of your Father and dare to embrace your position as a daughter of the King, you will begin to experience power in your prayers.

Think about the prayers you've been praying. Do they reflect God's call on your life? Are you letting others dictate God's purpose for you, or are you responding to Him directly? What needs to change in your life to bring your thoughts, attitudes, and actions in line with God's purpose and destiny for you?

Talk to God about these things.

CHAPTER 16

Praying in Harmony with Jesus (Revisited)

"That all of them may be one, Father, just as you are in me and I am in you. May they also be in us so that the world may believe that you have sent me."

— JOHN 17:21

I cannot say enough about prayer and intimacy with God, and this chapter continues my summary of previous chapters you have read.

Praying in the name of Jesus reflects our "oneness" with Him. God desires for us to be *one* with Him.

One mind
One heart
One spirit
One purpose
One life
One goal
One truth
One

What's in a Name?

The best way to describe what I mean when I say we must pray in harmony with Jesus is to call this oneness "intimacy" and liken it to what happens in our society when a man takes a woman to be his "lawfully wedded wife." Please humor me and allow me to share one more "for instance" from my own marriage.

When Tom and I married, I loved having those thank you cards that were engraved with "Mr. and Mrs. Thomas J. McCoy." I thought that was so cool! When I said, "I do," I willingly identified with Tom—became one with him, in a sense, by relinquishing my own name and receiving his. When I accepted Tom's marriage proposal, I gave up my right to be Leighann Keesee. On January 3, 1987, I became Leighann McCoy. All my legal documents changed, and my driver's license changed. I gave up Keesee and became McCoy; I chose to connect my life to Tom's name forevermore.

For the most part being connected to Tom's name has been a pleasure. I have a rich and wonderful heritage with my parents-in-law Dr. Don and Sterline McCoy. When I first moved to Tennessee, people all around said, "You're Dr. Don's daughter-in-law!" Or they said, "I know your mother-in-law, Sterline McCoy." Tom's father was a pastor in Dickson, Tennessee, for many years, and his parents had established a good name for us in middle Tennessee. Later on, after my father-in-law retired, I traveled across the state and people said, "You're Tom McCoy's wife." At times I am pleased to be known as "Mrs. Tom McCoy."

> When we pray in harmony with Jesus, we are relinquishing our own agendas for His alone.

Still, there are also times when being Mrs. Tom McCoy is difficult. During that season in the life of our church when people were confused and conflicted and there was bickering among our church body, I didn't much like being "Pastor Tom's wife." I would have rather been one of them and not had to deal with the junk they hurled at my husband. Because, however, I've chosen a life of oneness with Tom, I must suffer when he suffers and stand by his side when he is criticized. Occasionally I've agreed with his critics and had to keep my mouth shut and stand with him anyway!

When we pray in harmony with Jesus, we are praying in oneness with Him. We are marrying our desires to His good pleasure, and we are relinquishing our own agendas (our own names) for His alone. When Jesus responds to these prayers, we must also be careful to point the praise to whom it belongs and never consider ourselves worthy of such honor.

When Peter and John healed the lame man in the temple, they said, "Why are you amazed at this? Or why do you stare at us, as though by our own power or godliness we had made him walk? The God of Abraham, Isaac, and Jacob, the God of our fathers, has glorified His Servant Jesus" (Acts 3:12–13a HCSB).

Praying in harmony with Jesus is not only powerful but also precious. In that place of oneness we experience intimacy with our holy God, and in that intimacy we're lifted up where we can soar with eagles.

Harmony in the Band

I played the clarinet in my high school band. I was a fairly good clarinet player, and I actually enjoyed band. I loved being a part of the music and actually "felt" it when the brass section blew their horns, the percussion kept the beat, and the woodwinds joined in. But even if only one player in a section started playing the wrong thing, we didn't have harmony. We produced sounds that actually hurt not just our ears but our insides. When you play an instrument in a band, your part only matters when it is synchronized with the whole.

Sometimes our prayers lack power because they are not synchronized with the heart of God. We pray for the wrong things for the wrong reasons. We beg God to stop our pain when that very pain teaches us how to depend on Him. We ask Him to heal our loved ones when their death is their greatest reward. We want out of suffering when, certainly, the tears we shed water the parched soil of our worldly hearts and make them fertile ground for God's greater gifts.

Mudpies and Magpies

I can't shake the image of playing in the dirt. I know some people who have been playing in dirt piles so long that they are quite good at making mudpies. They've mastered forming those mudpies into works of art. But no matter how great their art might be, it will never compare to the real life God invites them to build. Not only that, but the rain will eventually come and the wind will blow and the pies they so lovingly formed will wash away to nothing. Mudpies simply cannot stand against the storms of life.

People who are unwilling to get out of the dirt might pray, but when they pray they ask God to keep the sun shining. They want the texture of the dirt just right so that their mudpies will be easier to form. They ask God to keep the storms at bay and get angry with Him when He doesn't save them from the wind and the rain and the hail and the flood and . . .

Too many times we think we are praying in harmony with Jesus when our prayers are childish whinings rooted in selfish ambition and worldly affection. God will rarely ever stoop down to help you build mudpies. If ever He does, you can be sure He's doing it so that you will get to know Him better and be willing to go with Him when He calls you to get out of your dirt. Daughters of the King were destined for much more than mud.

Similar to mudpies, considering magpies also forms a negative image. Magpies are birds that chatter much, and they have become synonymous with people who like to talk. Some people pray as magpies chatter. A magpie pray-er thinks she will somehow bend the ear of God by pestering Him into listening to the sound of her voice. Jesus taught in Matthew 6 that we won't get far in prayer by "babbling like pagans" (v. 7).

> God will rarely ever stoop down to help you build mudpies.

I laugh when I read this. I imagine how irritating it might be to listen to meaningless chatter that some people call prayer. I can't help but believe that God had been looking forward to the moment He could say this to us: "Stop babbling on and on when you pray! I'm truly listening, and it gets exhausting to hear you say nothing in so many words!"

Listen the next time you are with a group of people and they are praying out loud. Ask yourself this question: How would I know if God answered these prayers? We are notorious for praying phrases that protect God in case He doesn't do anything in response to our prayers. For example:

"Lord, bless the missionaries . . ."

"Father, give _____ comfort in her illness."

"Lord, we pray for the lost . . ."

"God, be glorified."

What do these prayers mean? How will we know when they are answered?

Not only that, but sometimes we pray our "to-do" list.

"Lord, help me to make that phone call to the doctor and to get that card in the mail and buy groceries today and . . ."

"Father, you know that we have over five thousand lost people in our community; save them, Lord."

Do we really need God's help to make a phone call? Does God need us to tell Him how many people are lost? Hasn't He already done what needs to be done to save them?

Sometimes we just start talking, and our prayers become nothing. If we toss in a few "Thee's" and "Thou's," we can almost sound poetic. But magpie prayer is not prayer that is in harmony with Jesus.

When Jesus prayed, He always prayed specific prayers whose answers could be readily seen.

You can only pray in harmony with Jesus when you choose to give up making mudpies and when you stop chattering like magpies. Once you recognize that God has called you to participate in the authority of Jesus—and when you understand that part of that authority includes the privilege of calling on the power of God in complete confidence that He will answer—then you will discover how to pray in harmony with Jesus.

Oh God, Please . . .

When we pray in harmony with Jesus, we are praying in oneness with Him. We are marrying our desires to His good pleasure, and we are relinquishing our own agendas (our own names) for His alone.

1. Consider the things you long for. What relationships are you asking God to mend? What needs do you have that you long for God to fill? Jot these things down.

2. Ask God to show you if your prayers line up with His purposes. Invite Him to tell you whether you are praying mudpie prayers when He is calling you out of the dirt.

3. Tell God that you want to live in the light of this truth: "For my thoughts are not your thoughts, neither are your ways my ways," declares the Lord. "As the heavens are higher than the earth, so are my ways higher than your ways and my thoughts than your thoughts" (Isaiah 55:8–9).

Pray: *Oh God, please line my prayers up with the heart and mind of Christ. Amen*

CHAPTER 17

Prayers that Are Sanctioned by Jesus (Revisited)

"You may ask me for anything in my name, and I will do it."

— JOHN 14:14

Praying in Jesus' name is like a filter: "Lord, hear me and take what I'm asking—rearrange it, change it, fix it so that You make it into what I really need."

When I was young I thought I knew so much. I knew what kind of man I wanted to marry, and if he wasn't already that way, once I married him I knew how to change him. I knew what I needed to make me happy, and when I got it I knew what else I needed to make me happier.

And I definitely knew that God meant for me to be happy. I wasn't ever the kind of young woman who thought that I knew better than God *how* to make me happy. I didn't ever turn my back on His Word and go with the world—not blatantly anyway. I didn't smoke or drink or cuss or date guys who did. I didn't sleep around, and I didn't take the Lord's name in vain.

> God will never do anything outside of His holiness and His righteousness.

Some of you may have done one or all of these things—either because you wanted to or because you didn't know any better. If you did, know that I am not about to tell you that because I didn't I am better than you—or my prayers are more likely to be answered than yours. Have no doubt, both you and I can become powerful prayer warriors!

You see, rather than stain my life with worldly living, I just formed God into the image I needed Him to be so that I could use Him as my "go-to" Guy for my own happiness.

And I prayed accordingly.

I've prayed a whole lot of prayers that were not sanctioned by Jesus. Had God granted the answers I wanted from those prayers, He would have acted against His own character. And God will never do anything outside of His holiness and His righteousness.

Me, Myself, and I

I live in Tennessee. When I moved here most of my neighbors were from Michigan because General Motors opened a plant in a nearby cornfield. Since I've been here I've asked God to move some people back north. I've asked Him to send others off the face of the earth. I figure He designed the law of gravity—He can just exempt some people from having to be bound by it.

But God never answered those prayers. He also never rushed my growing-up process. Many times I found myself in a difficult place due to my own ambition or poor judgment or insecurity or ferocious appetite for the grass that grew greener just on the other side of the fence. And I begged God to save me from myself. (That might have been one of the most unsanctioned prayers I ever prayed.)

Most often God let the consequences of my own choices play out in my life. He didn't rescue me from them. In fact God has always been far more patient with me than I am with myself, and He waits for quite a long time for me to grow.

As I've matured in my walk with the Lord, I have grown to appreciate the fact that I cannot manipulate or control God. I can ask. I can beg. I can even pitch a fit and baptize my prayers with countless Scripture promises, but I cannot *make* God do anything. I learned this lesson best when my friend Jenny died of cancer.

Jenny called me one day and told me that although she was the mother of three young children and in the first trimester of her pregnancy with her fourth, she wanted to start a ministry to young mothers. I met with her and was impressed with her enthusiasm. Jenny loved the Lord, she loved her children, and she was eager to do something great for His kingdom.

A few weeks after Jenny shared her dream, she was diagnosed with cancer. The thought of a young pregnant woman dying of cancer was beyond my definition of the goodness of God. So I (and eventually our entire congregation) prayed fervently that Jenny would not die.

Just a little more than two years later I stood at Jenny's bed and held hands with her family as her husband held her dead body in his arms and we sang hymns. Peace was in that bedroom, peace that swallowed the grief and the anger and the madness of Jenny's death. But on my way home from Jenny's house that night, I hollered at God.

I shouted that He made a mockery of us! As an entire congregation we prayed, we claimed Scripture, we anointed Jenny with oil, and we fasted. We believed, we worshipped, and we did everything He told us to do . . . but Jenny still died.

I was driving past the neighborhood I used to jog through when I put my anger into these words, "Lord, You have made me the prayer minister at this church and urged me to encourage the people to pray. You asked me to challenge them to believe that You are the same today as You were yesterday when You performed all kinds of miracles. Don't you understand how hard this is for me?! How am I supposed to defend Your glory when You didn't give us our miracle?!"

Now, because of my brazen prayer I don't know whether you are putting this book down right now and running far away just in case God strikes it with lightning, but don't worry—God let me live to pray another day.

The Corner Lighthouse

Before I relate what He spoke to me, I want to tell how we raised the money to build our first church building. When Tom and I came to Thompson's Station Baptist Chapel, our mother churches had helped our little congregation purchase a building in downtown Thompson's Station, which then consisted of a country market, a post office, and the building we met in. Downtown Thompson's Station has not changed much in more than twenty years. The country market is now a restaurant, and the post office houses part of our tiny city hall. The building that we owned is now the community center. It had been a honky tonk, kind of a weekend hangout for rednecks where bands played, people danced, and the bar served cheap beer.

The mother churches had also helped our little congregation purchase five acres of land on the main highway about a half mile from downtown. Because our little congregation had

> When we become too glib in prayer, we are most surely talking to ourselves.
> A. W. TOZER

been trying to become a real church for ten years, wise men advised Tom to move out of that building downtown (which could seat only one hundred people comfortably) and into a new building on the main road. The premise? If we built a "real" church building, the community would know that we were going to be a "real" church. Because Tom and I had not been a part of the ten-year history, we marched forward certain that we would have a new building on the main road.

To rally our weary troops, we made two lighthouses out of plywood. Tom told us a story about a lighthouse in one of his sermons. His story went something like this:

A lighthouse was built on a rocky shore where countless ships had wrecked and many lives had been lost. The people of the seaside community had decided that they wanted to do something about the loss of lives so they gave their money and time to build and staff the lighthouse.

Once the lighthouse was built, the ships that sailed nearby avoided the sharp rocks and shallow waters that had taken the lives of others. On the rare occasion that ships wrecked, the men of the community rescued those who were caught in the waters and brought them into the warmth of the lighthouse.

Through the years the people of the community added to the lighthouse property—a hospital and then a home for the widows of shipwrecked seamen. Their ministry to the men of the sea became known up and down the shore. Soon the original few who built the lighthouse left the town and went about speaking in other towns, telling them how they could build lighthouses too. Their travels brought more fame to the small community, and people from north and south all along the water's edge traveled to the community to visit the lighthouse.

The keepers of the lighthouse made improvements. Their success generated money, and they were able to decorate and make it the finest lighthouse in all the land. Many years went by, and no ships ever sank in the waters near this lighthouse. Rather than fill the hospital with wounded sailors, they transformed the rooms to classes where they got together and talked about the rescues that others made years ago.

On a very dark night, a large ship ran across the sharp rocks and began to sink, but no men who had ever actually been on a rescue mission still lived there. The only rescue boats they had were encased in museum displays. And when a few lucky sailors washed ashore, the keepers of the lighthouse didn't want to bring them in for fear they would soil the carpet or stain the beautiful furniture.

Our plywood lighthouses became symbols of the kind of church we wanted to be in Thompson's Station. We wanted to be a real lighthouse, one that pointed people to the Light of the world. And we were determined never to become like the lighthouse in Tom's story.

As we raised $127,000 to build our first "lighthouse" on that corner so near the highway, we painted stripes on the plywood lighthouses that we put in front of the congregation. When the plywood was painted, the money was collected.

Now back to the night that Jenny died and my self-focused prayer:

"Lord, You have made me the prayer minister at this church and urged me to encourage the people to pray. . . . How am I supposed to defend Your glory when You didn't give us our miracle?!"

God immediately gave me a picture in my mind of those plywood lighthouses, and this is what He said: "L.A. [that's what God calls me when I pray], what is the purpose of a lighthouse?"

"To save the ships?"

"Do lighthouses save ships?" God gently prodded.

"No, lighthouses simply shine the light into the darkness," I answered.

"Do they calm the raging seas?"

"No, Lord. Lighthouses simply shine the light so that those who are caught on the raging seas might avoid disaster." I began to understand.

"Is it your job to do more than that?"

"No, Lord."

God gently told me that I was not in the position to defend His glory. It was not my job to teach people to pray in such a way that they could guarantee themselves safe sailing. As the prayer minister at Thompson Station Church it was my job—my only job—to shine God's Light in the darkness. He went on to explain to me that storms would come and storms would go, but when the nights grow dark, His Light shines bright.

A bit later He quite explicitly explained to me that His glory is His very own and He doesn't need me to protect it—He is quite capable of doing that Himself.

Sometimes we pray and think that Jesus has sanctioned our prayers. But when they aren't answered the way we think they ought to be, we must acknowledge that God is God and we are not.

> When the nature of Jesus becomes your priority—the power of God will be unleashed through your prayers.

If you want a great reminder of this truth, read all of Isaiah 40 but particularly store away verses 27–28: "Why do you say, O Jacob, and complain, O Israel, 'My way is hidden from the Lord; my cause is disregarded by my God.' Do you not know? Have you not heard? The Lord is the everlasting God, the Creator of the ends of the earth. He will not grow tired or weary, and his understanding no one can fathom."

Sometimes I imagine God and Jesus listening intently to my prayers when suddenly God turns to Jesus and says, "Did she just say what I think she said? Surely she didn't mean it!"

Jesus smiles a tentative little grin then breaks into a laugh when He hears me say, *"In Jesus' name I pray, amen."* Immediately He turns to God and says, "I think this is what she meant . . ." And with that, long after I'm up and going about my day, Jesus and His loving Heavenly Father linger for hours discussing how best to respond to my heart's sometimes confused little plea.

Perhaps people today don't pray because they have neglected the key to unlocking power in prayer. The power of God is not available to you if you do not share the heart of God. As you grow in your prayer life and as you embrace the heart of God and the mind of Christ—when the nature of Jesus becomes your priority—the power of God will be unleashed through your prayers.

Oh God, Please . . . .

1. Have you ever had a time when God confused you by His response (or lack thereof) to your prayer?

2. How did you feel when that happened to you?

3. Have you ever looked back and discovered why God said no to one of your prayers?

4. Share what God taught you through that experience with a friend.

Pray: Talk to God about whatever is on your heart. *Father, please give me understanding so that I can begin to see how the answers to these prayers might bring You glory. Use me, if you see fit, to partner with You in bringing Your answers to my prayers. I am willing, and with Your help I know I am able. Amen*

PART 5

When You Pray . . .

Prayer is often expressed in word, but it is not
the words that God recognizes as prayer.
It is not the cry of the lips, but the cry of
the heart that God hears. We are living prayer.
Our lives are the aroma of Christ rising before
God continually as a sweet-smelling sacrifice.[4]

—

JENNIFER KENNEDY DEAN

CHAPTER 18

Prayer Is a Practice

[Jesus said,] "And when you pray . . ."

— MATTHEW 6:5

J esus' disciples noticed His ministry. Then, they noticed His practice of prayer. Prayer is most powerful when we practice it. My friends, the reason we see so little evidence of the power of God demonstrated in the lives of His people today is because God's people don't pray.

S. D. Gordon, a prolific writer and gentle speaker who ministered in the early twentieth century, wrote this:

> The great people of the earth today are the people who pray! I do not mean those who talk about prayer; nor those who say they believe in prayer; nor those who explain prayer; but I mean those who actually take the time to pray. They have not time. It must be taken from something else. That something else is important, very important and pressing, but still, less important and pressing than prayer. There are people who put prayer first and group the other items in life's schedule around and after prayer. These are the people today who are doing the most for God in winning souls, in solving problems, in awakening churches, in supplying both men and money for mission posts, in

keeping fresh and strong their lives far off in sacrificial service on the foreign field, where the thickest fighting is going on, and in keeping the old earth sweet a little while longer.

Teach Us to Pray

Disciples were common in Jesus' day. Men followed teachers to learn more from them. When Jesus' disciples watched Him perform miracles, cast out demons, and confound the religious leaders, they realized that His ministry was authenticated by the power of God. As they examined Jesus' life and compared Him to other teachers, they determined that the discipline that set Jesus apart from others was His practice of prayer. So they asked Him to teach them to pray.

The Lord's Prayer was first given when Jesus' disciples asked Him to teach them to pray. The concept of prayer was not new to Jesus' disciples. People had been praying for years. In fact, Jesus used some of those people as examples of how *not* to pray before He told His disciples how *to* pray.

The disciples did not ask Jesus to teach them to pray simply because they were curious. They asked Him because

> Prayer is most powerful when we practice it.

they'd witnessed the demonstration of God's power in Jesus' life. Jesus' disciples watched Him wander off by Himself early every morning, and they knew that He went to pray. Therefore, they surmised that a direct correlation existed between Jesus' prayer life and the demonstration of God's power in His public ministry.

The Lord's Prayer

In the next chapter I will take you step by step through the Lord's Prayer, but before Jesus gave His disciples the actual prayer, He said several things about praying.

When You Pray, Do Not Be Like the Hypocrites

"And when you pray, do not be like the hypocrites, for they love to pray standing in the synagogues and on the street corners to be seen by men. I tell you the truth, they have received their reward in full. But when you pray, go into your room, close the door and pray to your Father, who is unseen. Then your Father, who sees what is done in secret, will reward you" (Matthew 6:5–6).

> With God there is no *inner* man and *outer* man— there is simply man.

Before Jesus gave His disciples the Lord's Prayer, He discussed the difference between how He wanted His disciples to pray and the ways that others prayed. The first "others" He mentioned were the hypocrites.

Ben Patterson said, "The problem with praying as a hypocrite is that God can't be fooled."[5] Written on a block of wood and hanging in my family room is the quote, "You can fool all people some of the time, you can fool some people all of the time, but you can't fool mom!" God's like that too. We can't fool God.

With God there is no *inner* man and *outer* man—there is simply man. Remember what God said to Adam just after the fall? "Then the man and his wife heard the sound of the Lord God as he was walking in the garden in the cool of the day, and they hid from the Lord God among the trees of the garden. But the Lord God called to the man, 'Where are you?' He answered, 'I heard you in the garden, and I was afraid because I was naked; so I hid.' And He said, 'Who told you that you were naked?'" (Genesis 3:8–11a).

The Lord never saw Adam as "naked"—there was no distinction between what Adam looked like on the outside and what he looked like on the inside. When God walked in the garden, He only saw Adam as loved.

Consider Samuel's conversation with God when God sent him to anoint the next king of Israel. God had rejected Saul and sent Samuel to Bethlehem to find Jesse. He told Samuel that once he met Jesse He would then show Samuel which of Jesse's sons to anoint as king. "When they arrived, Samuel saw Eliab and thought, 'Surely the Lord's anointed stands here before the Lord.' But the Lord said to Samuel, 'Do not consider his appearance or his height, for I have rejected him. The Lord does not look at the things man looks at. Man looks at the outward appearance, but the Lord looks at the heart'" (1 Samuel 16:6–7).

If Samuel were left to his own observations, Eliab might have seized Israel's throne, and the nation wouldn't have been any better off with Eliab than they were with Saul.

The hypocrite can fool all the people some of the time, he can fool some of the people all the time, but he can't fool God! Hypocrisy is like magic—the hypocrite's actions are illusions; they *seem* to be genuine, but deep inside the hypocrite's heart lies motivation and intent that is far from sincere.

Jesus warned His disciples, "Do not be like the hypocrites."

The hypocrites prayed, they prayed often, and they prayed fervently. Their prayers were loud and fancy. They were pious and disciplined. The value of their prayers, however, was spent the moment their lips stopped moving. Why? Because the hypocrites were more interested in people hearing their prayers than they were in God hearing them pray.

The Psalmist understood this principle of prayer. He wrote,

> Who may ascend the hill of the Lord?
> Who may stand in his holy place?
> He who has clean hands and a pure heart.
> (Psalm 24:3–4a)

God sees the heart and weighs a man by what he hides within. Prayer is far more than words; it is far more than quoting memorized poems, far more than merely speaking. Your prayer life will grow powerful as your walk with Jesus grows intimate.

I wrote this definition for prayer in my book *Women Overcoming Fear*:

> David had a vital prayer life. What is that—a vital prayer life? It is worship, it is praise, it is time spent meditating on God's Word and reflecting on His goodness. A vital prayer life is discipline and desire; it is talking, dancing, singing, and crying. A vital prayer life is two-way communication; it is intimacy and delight.
>
> A vital prayer life is the lifeline of your relationship with God. It is the sum total of the way you develop your connection with Him while you are here on this crazy mixed-up swirling mass of matter we call earth.

While prayer is all these things, you can take some practical steps to get to this place. Jesus listed one of them here: "But

when you pray, go into your room, close the door and pray to your Father, who is unseen. Then your Father who sees what is done in secret, will reward you" (Matthew 6:6).

Besides resisting the temptation to try and impress others with your incredible spirituality, praying alone will also aid in focusing your thoughts on God, rather than your prayers. The enemy will still try to distract you when you pray, so ward off his distractions by creating a prayer space. I hope that by now you have already done this, but in case you haven't, a plan for creating a prayer place is in the appendix.

When you pray, go into your room, close the door, and be honest with your Father. Don't be like the hypocrites—you can't fool God.

> Your prayer life will grow powerful as your walk with Jesus grows intimate.

When You Pray, Do Not Keep on Babbling Like the Pagans
"And when you pray, do not keep on babbling like the pagans, for they think they will be heard because of their many words. Do not be like them, for your Father knows what you need before you ask him" (Matthew 6:7–8).

I have visited two pagan houses of worship. I told you about the Hindu temple in chapter 9. I can still hear the shouting and chanting and those bells ringing as the worshippers cried out to that golden idol in New Delhi.

The other temple I visited was a Buddhist one in Kyoto, Japan. I took a trip there with mothers and their daughters (ages ten to thirteen). Like the Hindu temple area, in Kyoto we walked past vendors who sold trinkets we could use in our prayers. We could purchase tiny stuffed animals, wooden plaques, and paper bookmarks, not to mention incense to burn at the altars.

Unlike the Hindu temple, this Buddhist place of worship was quiet and subdued. People paused to offer the little Buddha statue fruit and trinkets. They bowed and whispered prayers as they burned their incense. As I watched them I considered the difference between this pagan place and the other one I'd seen. One of the girls asked me if we could pray. I wondered why I hadn't thought of that and told her it was a great idea. We circled up right in front of Buddha's house and prayed that the pagans would come to know the only true and living God.

Pagans are sincere, unlike hypocrites, but they are sincerely wrong. And like the hypocrites, pagan prayers are void and without power. The Bible best demonstrates powerless pagan praying in Elijah's showdown with the prophets of Baal on Mt. Carmel. We read about this day in 1 Kings 18:25–29.

> They called to their false god and got no response.

Basically Elijah challenged Baal's prophets to a duel of sorts. He and they chose a bull and placed it on altars to Baal and to God. Elijah commended Baal's prophets for being great in number, and he told them to invite their god to light the fire that would burn their bull.

The prophets of Baal called on the name of Baal all morning, right up until noon. "Answer us, Baal!" they shouted, but even with their chorus of voices, Baal remained silent. So in the afternoon they danced. Baal's prophets danced around their bull and most likely twisted their bodies and contorted their limbs in an effort to please their god.

Elijah couldn't stand it; he started taunting them. "Shout louder!" he said. "Surely he is a god! Perhaps he is deep in thought, or busy, or traveling. Maybe he is sleeping and must be awakened." So they shouted louder and slashed themselves with swords and spears, as was their custom, until their blood flowed. Midday passed, and they continued their frantic prophesying until the time for the evening sacrifice. But there was no response, no one answered, no one paid attention" (1 Kings 18:27–29).

It seems Baal's prophets did everything right. They called on the name of their god, they called louder, and then they danced. The prophets worshipped in abandon, even to the extreme of drawing their own blood in their attempt to receive some response from Baal. But according to Scripture, "there was no response, . . . no one paid attention."

Baal's prophets were sincere, but they were sincerely wrong.

Jesus warned His disciples not to mimic the religious practices of pagan worshippers. He went on to explain why His followers' needn't be like them: "Your Father knows what you need before you ask Him" (Matthew 6:8b).

Many people fall far short of the power of prayer because they assume prayer is about letting God know what they want. Let that sink in a moment. How many times do we exhaust our emotional energy telling God how to fix our problems? How often do we cry out to Him just to let Him know what He needs to do in someone else's life?

I've learned a boatload of things these past few months, and one of them is: I am very patient with God's timeframe when it

> God already knows what we need, you just have to ask.

comes to Him teaching me truths I need to know, truths that will change me from who I am today to who I need to become, to be more like Christ. I am quick to excuse myself and learn to live with myself as I am.

But, when I present God with someone I need Him to change, I want Him to make that change quickly! I am not nearly as patient with the time it might take Him to change that other person. And I am really quite good at telling Him exactly how I want those changes to take place—tuck a little here, plump up a little there, shave off a little here, and get rid of that all together!

Many years ago I had an "ah ha" moment when I was writing the prayer study that this series of books will be taken from, *Oh God, Please! The Heart Cry of a Burdened Soul.* That moment came when I recognized an amazing truth woven throughout Scripture: God already knows what we need—and He longs to give His blessings, His power, His strength, His life to us! In fact, the three points I make in that prayer study are:

1. God is all powerful.
2. God's love is perfect in every way.
3. God longs to demonstrate His power and His love in and through our lives as we partner with Him in His kingdom work.

When you pray, don't be like the pagans, for your Father knows what you need before you ask. And often what you need is far different than what you are asking for. And besides that, when Jesus taught His disciples to pray, He didn't say, "Oh God, please let Your will be done *in heaven* to match my will *on earth*." Instead He prayed, "Thy will be done *on earth* as it is *in heaven*."

Oh God, Please . . .

Know this: your Father listens when you pray. He is eager to demonstrate His power and His love in and through your life. So find that quiet place, set aside that time, and begin your conversation with Him like this,

"Our Father which art in heaven, hallowed by thy name.
Thy kingdom come. Thy will be done in earth, as it is in heaven.
Give us this day our daily bread.
And forgive us our debts, as we forgive our debtors.
And lead us not into temptation, but deliver us from evil:
For thine is the kingdom, and the power, and the glory, for ever.
Amen. (Matthew 6:9–13 KJV)

CHAPTER 19

Our Father

"This, then, is how you should pray: 'Our Father . . .'"

— MATTHEW 6:9

God had already portrayed Himself throughout the Old Testament as a loving Father (Deuteronomy 32:6), as a faithful Husband (Hosea 3:1), and as a compassionate Lover (Song of Solomon 2:16). Never, though, did He express the full impact of our privileged position with Him as He did when Jesus taught His disciples to pray.

Father, Daddy! God! You see, the word *Abba* literally means, "Daddy." It's more than a title; it's a relationship. Prior to Jesus dying for our sins, this title would have never been considered appropriate for man to use when referring to Jehovah God. God uses this title in reference to Himself as He describes His relationship with us, but it is presumptuous for us to use it when referring to our relationship with Him.

When Jesus prayed in the garden of Gethsemane, He went beyond the more formal "Father" to an intimate, taking-His-Father's-face-in-His-hands-beseeching plea. "Abba! Father! All things are possible for You; remove this cup from Me; yet not what I will, but what You will" (Mark 14:36 NASB).

"Daddy, oh Daddy!"

Jesus came to share sonship with us. Paul said, "The Spirit Himself bears witness with our spirit that we are children of God, and if children, then heirs—heirs of God and joint heirs with Christ" (Romans 8:16–17 NKJV).

When Jesus taught His disciples to pray, He invited them (and us) to share His intimate relationship with His Father.

No longer do we need to slaughter goats, lambs, or pigeons to approach God's throne. No longer do we have to run and hide from His Presence (like Adam and Eve did when the shame of sin first reared its ugly head). Now, we have full access to the throne of grace, so we can approach boldly! "Let us then approach the throne of grace with confidence, so that we may receive mercy and find grace to help us in our time of need" (Hebrews 4:16).

My children do not hesitate to ask me *anything*. They are completely confident in my unconditional love for them. They are also confident in my vast resources. While I am certainly not as wealthy as some, I do have more than my children—and they have no problem understanding that what is mine is theirs for the asking!

> We have full access to the throne of grace, so we can approach boldly!

God wants us to understand this Father/child relationship. He wants us to wrap our finite minds around the infinite wonder of this: He is the perfect Father. God is our Father by creation; He is also our Father by covenant relationship.

God made us, ("The Lord God formed the man from the dust of the ground and breathed into his nostrils the breath of life, and the man became a living being" [Genesis 2:7]).

And He chose us. ("For He chose us in Him before the creation of the world to be holy and blameless in His sight" [Ephesians 1:4]).

Because we belong to God, because we are loved by Him and are the recipients of His vast resources, we are invited to come to Him with the boldness of a child who eagerly climbs into the lap of his loving Father, snuggles close, and whispers in His ear exactly what rests in his heart.

I saw this truth beautifully illustrated one day while I was working out at the YMCA. In our kick-boxing class, we jiggled our thighs in front of a wall of windows. Sometimes I laugh out loud at what the passersby must have thought as they watched us kick and punch thin air. But somehow when you're in a group of people, and all of you are doing the same silly thing, that silly thing doesn't seem quite so silly after all! I don't know if they enjoyed looking in, but just like the monkeys in the zoo, I enjoyed looking out. It kept my mind off of breathing.

One day I looked out the window and saw a woman with her hands cupped walking toward the bench (also like the zoo, the YMCA had benches for those who wanted to pause and watch us longer). Right on her heels were two small children, a girl and a boy. The boy had his hands cupped just like his mother's, but there was nothing in his hands. As soon as their mother sat down, the little girl crawled right up next to her, intent on whatever was in her mom's hands. The little boy kept his hands cupped and reached them up to her while she sat counting.

> God holds everything we need to live our lives victoriously in a sin-stained world.

It was then I realized what this mother had in her hands, for several years ago, I had done the exact same thing. I had put a quarter in the Skittle machine, collected my handful, then equally distributed the colorful treats to each of my children. This mama was getting ready to meet a "need."

As I watched her, I thought, *Isn't this a great picture of what God is like?* When Jesus taught us to pray, He said, "This, then, is how you should pray: 'Our Father . . .'" Scripture tells us to approach God with the boldness of a child who is embraced by the love of his Father.

Scripture also tells us that God will supply *all* our needs according to His riches in heaven! In other words, God's hands are full! He doesn't hold Skittles in His hand; He holds blessings much more powerful. God holds healing, restoration, peace, contentment, security, and everything else we need (glorious riches of our inheritance) to live our lives victoriously in a sin-stained world. And when we pray, we are like those little children. Because we *know* He holds those things in His hands for us, we cup our little hands together as well and reach up to Him, fully expecting to receive the portion He sees fit to give to us.

It is deception of the worst kind to think God is waiting for us to impress Him in order to bless us. It is deception of the worst kind to think God has all this but refuses to give it to us. God *wants* to answer our prayers! He sent His precious Son, the crown Prince of heaven to earth to suffer and die so that we could have access to Him. That's why Jesus said, "This, then, is how you should pray: 'Our Father . . .'"

Oh God, Please . . .

1. Read Revelation 4:1–11 aloud.

2. Imagine God sitting on His throne.

3. Speak the angels' words to Him: "You are worthy, our Lord and God, to receive glory and honor and power, for you created all things, and by your will they were created and have their being" (Revelation 4:11).

Pray: Tell God how you feel about being able to call Him Father.

CHAPTER 20

Which Art in Heaven

"Our Father which art in heaven . . . ."

— MATTHEW 6:9B KJV

In his book *The Slumber of Christianity*, Ted Dekker says that Christians have lost their vision of heaven. While Jesus spent much of His teaching ministry painting a picture of our eternal home and encouraging us to embrace the privilege of our citizenship there, most American Christians have allowed the pleasures of this world to choke out the reality of heaven.

When Jesus taught His disciples to pray, He encouraged them to reflect on God's dwelling place. Prayer involves initiative in separating yourself from this life and focusing your attention on the life you were created to live—life in the presence of God! The psalmist demonstrated this particular aspect of prayer:

> *Surely goodness and love will follow me all the days of my life, and I will dwell in the house of the Lord forever. (Psalm 23:6)*

> *Better is one day in your courts than a thousand elsewhere; I would rather be a doorkeeper in the house of my God than dwell in the tents of the wicked. (Psalm 84:10)*

> *I rejoice with those who said to me, "Let us go to the house of the Lord." (Psalm 122:1)*

Welcome Home

God blessed me with Christian parents who took me to church from the time I was old enough to stay in the nursery. We were serious Christians, for we attended church Sunday morning, Sunday night, and Wednesdays! I can't remember when I first learned "God is love," nor do I remember when I first heard about heaven. But this I know: when I was about eight years old, I understood that unless I invited Jesus into my heart, I would not go to heaven when I died. And although death seemed a long way off (still does), I didn't like the uncertainty of not knowing what might happen to me on the other side of the grave.

> Prayer involves focusing your attention on living in the presence of God!

From the time I was eight until I was eleven, I wrestled with God. It wasn't that I didn't want to go to heaven when I died; it was that I didn't want to "walk the aisle" in my church. Back then our tradition was for new believers to leave their seats while the congregation sang, walk alone to the front of the room, take the hand of the pastor, and tell him that you wanted to be "saved." This was called "the invitation." Some churches still practice the invitation in their worship services today.

More than that, however, I wasn't sure I was ready to give my life over to God. I was independent, and even as a child I kind of liked that independence. Because I listened when my Sunday school teachers taught me the lessons, I knew that not only did Jesus die for my sins so that He could take me to heaven when I died, but He also wanted to be "Lord" of my life. That meant He wanted to be boss—and His being boss when I was eleven meant that I would have to "walk that aisle."

But on a Thursday night at Camp Pinnacle while a missionary sang "O Holy Night," God opened my spiritual eyes. I saw His love for me and understood I no longer wanted to live without Him. I invited Jesus into my heart. I asked Him to forgive me of my sins. I accepted His gift of salvation when He died *for me* on the cross, and I *knew* He'd take me to heaven when I died.

I cannot describe to you how amazingly happy that made me. To *know* I will live in the house of the Lord *forever!* No longer was I plagued by the fear of death and the unknown of the grave. But not only was I not afraid, I was also excited. The very prospect of heaven thrilled my soul! The next Sunday, I experienced my first step of obedience when I made the move from my pew and experienced the Holy Spirit empower me to "walk that aisle." For several months I fervently read every Scripture passage that talked about heaven. I drank in Revelation (although I didn't even try to understand the symbolism there) and longed for Jesus to return any minute.

But something happened with the passing of time. My anticipation and thrill of heaven waned, and I became much more interested in the present help of God than in the future hope of heaven. I would dare say that I am not alone. Most believers I know would most likely agree with me. The "foretaste of glory divine" becomes the glory divine if we don't make a concerted effort to focus our eyes on heaven.

When Jesus taught us to pray, He reminded us that our Father resides in heaven, and if that is where my Father lives, that is my home too.

Oh God, Please . . .

1. Read Revelation 22:1–7.

2. Describe heaven to a friend.

Pray: *Lord, thank You for promising to return for us soon. These are the things that I am passionate about . . . [share your passions and affections with God]. Lord, give me a glimpse of what my life might be like if earth was all that I had. Thank You that it is not. Help me to live with the ever-present understanding that heaven is better.*

CHAPTER 21

Hallowed Be Thy Name

"Our Father which art in heaven, hallowed be thy name."

—MATTHEW 6:9 KJV

J esus invited us to draw near to His Father's throne of grace with the trust and confidence of a child. Then, He reminded us to hallow His holy name. This hallowing of the name of the Lord is missing from our culture today.

Hallowed is the same word that is translated "sanctified." The word refers to the glory and magnitude of God. When Jesus urged us to hallow God's name, He urged us to pause in our prayers to ponder the wonder of God's character. A great practice of prayer is to consider all the names of God as referenced throughout Scripture. God makes Himself known by His names. Consider these:

- Wonderful, Blessed Redeemer
- Beautiful Savior and Friend
- Lamb of God; Prince of Peace; Immanuel
- Lord of lords and King of kings
- Righteous One; Holy and Sovereign; Creator; Ruler of all creation; Comforter; the Beginning and the End

Then and Now

When the Israelites followed God out of Egypt and into the wilderness, they understood the meaning of hallowing His name. They worshipped in the shadow of His presence as manifested in fire and clouds. They understood that if they overstepped their boundaries, they would be killed. (Even then they sometimes stepped over those lines.) But today we have so focused our attention on the grace and mercy of God that we have inadvertently reduced Him to the "Big Man Upstairs." What heresy!

I am amazed at the audacity we have to shake our little fists heavenward and blame God for pain and suffering when we arrogantly live our lives of sin as if He were not the least bit interested in our behavior. Oh, most people understand that Jesus suffered and died for us, but our attitudes are often, "Why not? After all, He loves us—and we deserve His love."

Several years ago I taught the sophomore Sunday school class at church, and although I didn't want to judge them harshly, it seemed to me that they brought that why-not attitude with them to church on Sunday morning. These young people—with bright futures and countless opportunities—came to class each week with no anticipation of learning anything they didn't already know. At the ages of fifteen and sixteen, they'd already dismissed God's eagerness to rule in their lives as something for only the serious Christians. For them, His death on the cross and their acceptance of it ended when they were dunked in the baptismal waters. As for His expectation to line their lives up in obedience to His Word, they seemed to embrace this philosophy: "Oh well, He'll understand. I'm forgiven."

> When you pray, draw near to the throne of grace with the innocent trust of a child.

Perhaps this attitude prevails in our teenagers because we've spent far too much time focusing on the mercy and grace of God and far too little time focusing on the glory of His name.

Hallowed be thy name . . .

What might happen if we hallowed His name in our worship services? What might happen if we paused from our productions long enough to stand in awe of His powerful presence? What might happen if we considered the awesome wonder of His might, the wonder the psalmist considered:

> The waters saw you, O God,
> the waters saw you and writhed;
> the very depths were convulsed.
> The clouds poured down water,
> the skies resounded with thunder;
> your arrows flashed back and forth.
> Your thunder was heard in the whirlwind,
> your lightning lit up the world;
> the earth trembled and quaked.
> Your path led through the sea,
> your way through the mighty waters,
> though your footprints were not seen."
> (Psalm 77:16–19)

Hallowed be thy name . . .

What might happen if we hallowed His name in our homes? What might happen if we truly understood that God sees us when no one else does, and He constantly considers our progression toward becoming vivid reflections of His Son? How might we address one another? As parents, would we seize every opportunity to point our children toward God?

Hallowed be thy name . . .

What might happen if we hallowed His name in our workplaces and schools? How often might we bear witness to others as His grateful sons and daughters? What temptations might we avoid? What conversations might we walk away from?

When you pray, draw near to the throne of grace with the innocent trust of a child. Look around that throne and realize His home will one day be your home too. Then focus your eyes on His face and hallow His name. When you hallow His name, you might just slip out of your Father's lap and onto the floor at His feet. You might bow low in reverence, in awe and wonder that the God of the universe chooses to be the Lover of your soul.

> *I saw the Lord seated on a throne, high and exalted, and the train of his robe filled the temple. Above him were seraphs, each with six wings: With two wings they covered their faces, with two they covered their feet, and with two they were flying. And they were calling to one another:*
>
> *"Holy, holy, holy is the Lord Almighty; the whole earth is full of His glory."*
>
> *At the sound of their voices the doorposts and thresholds shook and the temple was filled with smoke. "Woe to me!" I cried. "I am ruined! For I am a man of unclean lips, and I live among a people of unclean lips, and my eyes have seen the King, the Lord Almighty." (Isaiah 6:1–5)*

Hallowed be thy name.

Oh God, Please . . .

1. Go back through the "Hallowed be thy name" sections of this chapter. Answer the questions either privately in your prayer journal or with a group of friends.

2. Read Isaiah 6:1–5 aloud and imagine what you might have felt had you been standing with Isaiah.

3. Have you ever had an encounter with God that was overwhelming? If so, share that with a friend (or your book study group).

Pray: *Thank You, Lord, for bending down to us, and for never compromising Your glory when You do that. I understand that You stoop down to work in our lives. Thank You for Your willingness. I am yielded to You. I want to be easy to work with. Amen*

CHAPTER 22

Thy Kingdom Come.
Thy Will Be Done in Earth,
as It Is in Heaven

"Our Father which art in heaven, hallowed be thy name. Thy kingdom come. Thy will be done in earth, as it is in heaven."

—MATTHEW 6:9–10 KJV

Remember that the Lord's Prayer is an "index prayer," a model, a template. Jesus' intent was that His disciples would use the prayer's principles to guide their own variations of it as they prayed consistently throughout their lives.

Therefore, it is not by chance that He taught us that this should be our first petition. Rather than asking for material blessing or forgiveness of sin, Jesus encouraged us to first ask God to exert His authority and power in our world in the same way that His power is demonstrated in heaven.

Whimsy Is Flimsy

This is perhaps the greatest omission in our prayer lives—too often we ask God to allow our whims to rule in heaven rather than His power to rule on earth. Too many Christians approach God as if He's the acquisitions center and they are ready for their orders to be filled: "Father, I want my children to obey me, my husband to make more money, my projects to be successful, and Grandma's tumor to disappear." While these petitions are not all together petty, they do reflect our perception of what is "good" on earth. Without even considering how our lives, our suffering, or our circumstances might be used for the glory of God, we allow our inner drive for lives of ease to direct our requests.

Part of the reason Christians have difficulty experiencing powerful prayer is that they don't understand this principle. Prayer is *not* about us *getting* stuff from God. Prayer is *not* about us being rescued from every natural consequence of our sin. Prayer is *not* a tool to be used in our American pursuit of happiness. Prayer is about God's power reigning supreme in and through the lives of His children so that the world will recognize Him rising above the muck and mire of this sin-filled life.

This is the message of the first prayer study I wrote, *Oh God, Please! The Heart Cry of a Burdened Soul.* The study began where most of us are compelled to learn to pray. We come to the Lord eager to experience prayer when we are hurting, when we long for His intervention in our suffering, or when we want something we can't quite grasp. I grow most in my prayer life when I am living smashed in between the promises of God and my circumstances.

When Jesus walked on earth, these same things drew people to Him. They were

> God demonstrated His power and His love in and through Jesus' life.

blind, crippled, suffering from disease, caught in their sin, or even dead. Jesus met them at their point of need, but He didn't stop there. When Jesus healed the sick and made the lame to walk, the blind to see, and the deaf to hear, He did so to demonstrate the power of God. And through all His miraculous activity Jesus taught us that God longs to have a personal, dynamic relationship with Him. In *Oh God Please, Help Me with My Doubt* I take the reader from this stepping-on place (a burdened soul) to the linking-arms-and-hearts place of understanding in which God *longs* to demonstrate His power and His love in our lives *as we partner with Him* in His kingdom work.

Partnership with God is key to powerful prayer. God demonstrated His power and His love in and through Jesus' life because Jesus partnered perfectly with Him in His kingdom work.

As I teach on prayer, I remind people that God answers pray-ers (people who pray) not prayers (words that are prayed). Jesus taught us this when He said, "If you remain in me and my words remain in you, ask whatever you wish, and it will be given to you" (John 15:7). He told us that His works came directly from His Father. "By myself I can do nothing; I judge only as I hear, and my judgment is just, for I seek not to please myself but him who sent me" (John 5:30). "Jesus said, 'When you have lifted up the Son of Man, then you will know that I am the one I claim to be and that I do nothing on my own but speak just what the Father has taught me. The one who sent me is with me; he has not left me alone, for I always do what pleases him'" (John 8:28–29).

Praying with a sincere desire for God's will and not our own is absolutely essential to experiencing God in the conversation. Without this ambition we are merely talking to ourselves. Perhaps our prayer lives seem null and void because we have neglected this prayer: "*Thy* kingdom come. *Thy* will be done in earth, as it is in heaven."

Oh God, Please . . .

1. Consider your deepest desires. Do they reflect God's heart?

2. Consider your most recent prayer request. What makes that request something you long to see God answer?

3. What most often motivates your prayers?

4. How might your request change to reflect a genuine commitment to God's kingdom plan and not your own?

Pray: *Father, I invite the Holy Spirit to adjust my heart cries so that they mirror Your own. Amen*

CHAPTER 23

Give Us This Day Our Daily Bread

"Our Father which art in heaven, hallowed be thy name. Thy kingdom come. Thy will be done in earth, as it is in heaven. Give us this day our daily bread."

— MATTHEW 6:9-11 KJV

When Jesus taught His disciples to request their daily bread from God, in essence He was saying God cared for them. This applies to you as well. God cares if you're hungry, if you're sick, if you're lonely, if you're happy, and if you're sad. God cares that you have food and shelter. God cares for you because He loves you. God cares for you because He promised to, and God cares for you because you ask Him to.

My children are all three teenagers. They are at the age where they begin to sense that there is some kind of obligation on my part (apparently without any on theirs). I'm teaching them that we are all obligated to one another. Although I am somewhat wistful regarding the fact that within only a few short years they will no longer live in my home, I am preparing them for that day. We have conversations that sound like this: "Your room is your own. I want you to treat it with respect, and I will honor your space and your privacy. As your parents, your father and I are fully responsible for feeding you, clothing you, and providing you with shelter. We do these things because we love you and because we are your parents. But once you grow up, leave home to attend college, and begin to be 'on your own,' remember this: you are welcome to come back home—

even to live here for a time—but when that time comes (after you graduate from college), we will charge you rent for your room. For when you are an adult, we are no longer obligated to provide these things for you. That's part of growing up."

While that is good parenting, it's not exactly how Jesus told us our heavenly Father is. In the Lord's Prayer, Jesus encouraged us to ask God for our daily bread. As our loving Father, God's intent is to take care of us from this day forward and forever more. Note what James told us about this very thing: "You want something but don't get it. You kill and covet, but you cannot have what you want. You quarrel and fight. *You do not have, because you do not ask God*" (James 4:2, italics added). God longs to give good gifts to His children. Paul wrote, "He who did not spare his own Son, but gave him up for us all—how will he not also, along with him, graciously give us all things?" (Romans 8:32).

> God cares for you because He loves you. God cares for you because He promised to.

Blessed to Then Bless

God's love for you was demonstrated with extravagance. He gave His only begotten Son to redeem your soul from death—to draw you into a personal, dynamic relationship with Himself. How will He not eagerly address your basic needs?!

I love the story of George Muller. After stealing from his father and his friends, cheating and participating in all kinds of sinful behavior as an adolescent and young adult, George experienced radical transformation when he realized that only God could satisfy. As he grew in his faith, George came to the conviction that God, not man, would supply his needs. And so, he took Jesus' instructions to pray for his daily bread literally. And without ever making his needs known to man, George prayed and trusted God to meet his daily needs. He is best remembered for the orphanages that spread over thirteen acres in Bristol, England. He started these homes with only two shillings in his pocket (50 cents), and without making his needs known to man, more than £1,400,000 ($7 million) was sent to him for the building and maintenance of the orphanage.

George Muller embraced this prayer for his daily bread:

> Muller's health declined in London and his soul was also now on fire for God in such a way that he could not settle down to the routine of daily studies. His newly acquired belief in the near coming of Christ also urged him forward to work for the salvation of souls. He felt that the Lord was leading him to begin at once the Christian work he was longing to do, and as the London Missionary Society did not see proper to send him out without the prescribed course of training, he decided to go at once and trust the Lord for the means of support. Soon after this he became pastor of Ebenezer Chapel, in Teignmouth, Devonshire. His marriage to Miss Mary Groves, a Devonshire lady, followed. She was always of the same mind as her husband and their married life was a very happy one. Not long after his marriage he began to have conscientious scruples

about receiving a regular salary, and also about the renting of pews in his church. He felt that the latter was giving the "man with the ring on his finger" the best seat, and the poorer brother the footstool, and the former was taking money from those who did not give "cheerfully" or "as the Lord had prospered them." These two customs were discontinued by him. He and his wife told their needs to no one but the Lord. Occasionally reports were spread that they were starving; but though at times their faith was tried, their income was greater than before. He and his wife gave away freely all that they had above their present needs, and trusted the Lord for their "daily bread." [6]

When I was young I spent a week every summer with my grandparents. Papa Smith read the Bible daily and prayed this blessing over every meal: "Lord, bless the bereaved and the poor and the less fortunate than we." I'll never forget those words. I always ate far more than my fair day's portion when my grandma fed me. I never felt a hunger pain while I was in her home. But Papa's blessing always reminded me that life was not as bountiful for everyone. When I consider Jesus' instructions for us to pray for our *daily* bread, I wonder whether He was also reminding us that when the Lord sees fit to give us more than we need, perhaps He intends for us to "bless those less fortunate than we" with the leftovers!

For two reasons modern-day Christians have a difficult time truly understanding this part of the Lord's Prayer. First, we rarely have a need for God to meet! With grocery stores in every community and an abundance of money to purchase an abundance of food, we are rarely, if ever, hungry. Most of us are trying *not* to eat rather than wondering where our next meal will come from!

Second, few of us find ourselves satisfied with only a daily portion. Our security and comfort levels are only satisfied when we have enough for the foreseeable future. We want far more than today's portion. Too often we horde tomorrow's and next week's portions so that we can avoid finding ourselves in the desperate place of depending on God for only today's portion. The part of George Muller's story that impressed me was that he and his wife were so willing to take God at His Word that they gave away the next day's portion to others who needed it worse than they did. The Mullers trusted God for their daily bread.

Can you honestly pray, "Give us this day our daily bread," and mean it? Can you trust God to care for you? Do you believe that He already does? Can you ask Him for today's portion only? Are you OK with waiting until tomorrow to ask Him for just what you need then? Would you be willing to give the leftovers to others?

"Give us this day our daily bread"—it's a request filled with trust, it's a statement of faith, and it's a commitment to be generous to those less fortunate than we are.

Oh God, Please . . .

1. Have you ever visited a place where people live in poverty? If so, tell someone how that affected you.

2. Do you depend on God for your physical needs?

3. What might your life look like if you did depend on God to meet your daily needs?

4. How might you adjust the management of your money to honor God and this part of the Lord's Prayer?

5. Consider George Muller's life. Could you ever live like that?

Pray: Talk to God about your dependence on Him.

CHAPTER 24

And Forgive Us Our Debts, as We Forgive Our Debtors

"Our Father which art in heaven, hallowed be thy name. Thy kingdom come, Thy will be done in earth, as it is in heaven. Give us this day our daily bread. And forgive us our debts, as we forgive our debtors."

— MATTHEW 6:9–12 KJV

In one translation of the Bible, this sentence is, "Forgive us our trespasses as we forgive those who trespass against us." Remember the children's prayers in an earlier chapter and the young child who heard this phrase and proudly recited his version of it: "Forgive us our trash baskets as we forgive those who put trash in our baskets." Not a bad translation, huh?

Jesus taught us to ask our Father to forgive us our debts. This implies that our thoughts, attitudes, and actions have the power to offend the holiness and righteousness of God, leaving us with enormous debt when we approach His throne to make our requests.

Forgive us our debts—God's Word teaches us that God readily answers this prayer and includes the following three verses: "And everyone who calls on the name of the Lord will be saved" (Joel 2:32a); "And everyone who calls on the name of the Lord will be saved" (Acts 2:21); "For, 'Everyone who calls on the name of the Lord will be saved'" (Romans 10:13).

This reminds me of what many mothers have said through the ages: "I've told you once; I've told you twice; I've told you three times!" And when they say that, they are telling their children that their words are not once, not twice, but three times true. All of Scripture teaches that we serve a holy, righteous, all-powerful God who is eager to forgive us our debts. He is not a god who holds grudges; He is not a god who waits on sacrifice to appease His anger for our sin. He is the God who forgives those who trust and cry out to Him. "For he will deliver the needy who cry out, the afflicted who have no one to help. He will take pity on the weak and the needy and save the needy from death. He will rescue them from oppression and violence, for precious is their blood in his sight" (Psalm 72:12–14).

And while God is ready to forgive, our sin did cost Him dearly. With great love and compassion God satisfied His holiness in the suffering of His Son's crucifixion. God sent Jesus to pay the sacrifice of our sin. Jesus came to earth, walked among us, demonstrated God's power in His perfect life, then obediently accepted God's purpose for Him and became sin for us.

> All of Scripture teaches that we serve a holy, righteous, all-powerful God who is eager to forgive us our debts.

Paul wrote this about Jesus' life and death—His purpose fulfilled and the blessing of forgiveness available to man:

> *He is the image of the invisible God, the firstborn over all creation. For by him all things were created: things in heaven and on earth, visible and invisible, whether thrones or powers or rulers or authorities; all things were created by him and for him. He is before all things, and in him all things hold together. And he is the head of the body, the church; he is the beginning and the firstborn*

from among the dead, so that in everything he might have the supremacy. For God was pleased to have all his fullness dwell in him, and through him to reconcile to himself all things, whether things on earth or things in heaven, by making peace through his blood, shed on the cross. (Colossians 1:15–20)

God's nature is to forgive sin. Our nature is to need His forgiveness. So, Jesus taught us to ask for God's forgiveness when we pray.

However, don't miss the full impact of Jesus' instructions. The request is this: "Forgive us our debts, as we forgive our debtors." A partnership exists between God's willingness to forgive us and our willingness to forgive others. Forgiveness is a both/and activity. While we will offend God with our sin, others will also offend us with their sin. Have you been offended? Has someone you love hurt you? Have you been on the receiving end of another's poor attitudes or actions? No doubt you have!

You are not only in need of forgiveness; you are also in need of being forgiving. This is the only part of the Lord's Prayer that Jesus expounded on: "For if you forgive men when they sin against you, your heavenly Father will also forgive you. But if you do not forgive men their sins, your Father will not forgive your sins" (Matthew 6:14–15).

> You are not only in need of forgiveness; you are also in need of being forgiving.

Why did Jesus feel He needed to give further details about this part of the prayer? Was it because He knew this would be the one little snag we would have in experiencing victory in our prayer lives? Did He somehow know that we would be quick to ask for God's forgiveness but that we would also be easily offended and slow to offer forgiveness to others?

Too often God's children buy into the lie that as long as they are good with God they don't have to worry so much about being good with others. I know many men and women who worship on Sundays and even teach the Word but then live their lives loaded down with all kinds of offenses and grudges, carefully nurturing those bitter roots until they grow into a tangled mess. Jesus taught that if we live our lives in such a way we might think we've been forgiven, but as long as we're harboring unforgiveness in our own hearts, God will not release His forgiveness toward us. My friends, this is a dangerous way to live.

Several years ago some people in our church terribly slandered my husband. He was accused of all kinds of behavior that never even entered his mind to perform! We were caught off guard by these accusations and terribly wounded by the bickering and secret meetings several church members participated in. After two years, God ceased the trouble and established unity in our congregation. God allowed revival to begin, and we've remained in that place ever since—we've enjoyed a church where we are more interested in sharing Jesus with our community and world than we are in who gets the credit.

God took care of our problems, and my husband immediately moved forward. He chose to forget what lies behind and press on; however, I wasn't ready to let go. While I claimed Exodus 14:14 during the battle (and allowed God to teach me all kinds of things about prayer), once the victory was won I decided to replay what people had said and done. I wanted to harbor the offenses. I had a hard time rejoicing over the current activity because I was caught in the hurt of the past.

A friend gave me John Bevere's book *The Bait of Satan*, and as I read his book, I learned that I'd been snagged. Satan baited me by allowing me to be offended. While I did well behaving like a good child of God during the battle, I took hold of Satan's bait and gave free rein to bitterness as it inched its way deep in my spirit.

I did not move beyond the trouble in our church until I was willing to let go of those who'd hurt me by slandering my husband. I did not experience victory and joy until I was willing to let go of my bitterness and honestly forgive them for hurting me. Once I came to the place of forgiveness, I realized the great power of releasing the offenses of others. I realized that as I released them Satan's stronghold grew weak, and he was forced to release me. Only then did I experience what others were experiencing all around me—the joy of the Lord!

> *"Forgive us our debts, as we also have forgiven our debtors. . . . For if you forgive men when they sin against you, your heavenly Father will also forgive you. But if you do not forgive men their sins, your Father will not forgive your sins." (Matthew 6:12, 14–15)*

Even recently I had to go through this process. Before I could let my offender off the hook, I felt distant from God and spent a whole lot of my prayer time being tossed about on waves of doubt. After I let it go, however, and after I let the one who hurt me go, I began to see God answer my prayers. He didn't answer them the way I thought He would, but He did even more miraculous things in my relationship with my offender. This doesn't always occur, but it sure is great when it does!

Oh God, Please . . .

1. Ask God if there is unforgiveness in you. If there is, let it go.

2. Share with your friends a time when you harbored unforgiveness. Tell them how that made you feel. What thoughts filled your mind? Did you ever come to a place where you willingly forgave that person? If so, how did you get there?

3. Consider a time when you forgave someone who offended you. What happened once you forgave them?

Pray: *Father, I want to speak the language of heaven: forgiveness. But it is a language that my flesh despises. I choose to crucify my flesh and embrace Your command for me to forgive— over and over again. Lord, show me who I need to "let off the hook." I choose to forgive. Amen*

CHAPTER 25

And Lead Us Not into Temptation, but Deliver Us from Evil

"Our Father which art in heaven, hallowed be thy name. Thy kingdom come. Thy will be done in earth, as it is in heaven. Give us this day our daily bread. And forgive us our debts, as we forgive our debtors. And lead us not into temptation, but deliver us from evil."

— MATTHEW 6:9–13A KJV

After praying that God will forgive us our debts, Jesus then led us to ask Him to "lead us not into temptation." In other words, "Lord, forgive me for the things I've done wrong, and please help me never to do them again!" Matthew Henry said this:

> Having prayed that the guilt of sin may be removed, we pray, as it is fit, that we may never return again to folly, that we may not be tempted to it. It is not as if God tempted any to sin; but, "Lord, do not let Satan loose upon us; chain up that roaring lion, for he is subtle and spiteful; Lord, do not leave us to ourselves (Ps. 19:13), for we are very weak; Lord, do not lay stumbling-blocks and snares before us, nor put us into circumstances that may be an occasion of *falling*." Temptations are to be prayed against, both because of

the discomfort and trouble of them, and because of the danger we are in of being overcome by them, and the guilt and grief that then follow.

Who has not been overcome by temptation? Which one among us has not known the utter defeat of the enemy's subtle deceptive ways?

When I was a young teen, my pastor challenged us to memorize 1 Corinthians 10:13: "No temptation has seized you except what is common to man. And God is faithful; he will not allow you to be tempted beyond what you can bear. But when you are tempted, he will also provide a way out so that you can stand up under it." Once I learned this verse, I started looking for that way out!

Often those of us who have accepted God's gift of salvation forget that with eternal life also comes the power to overcome sin. We will not only go to heaven when we die but we also have

> Often we forget that with God's gift of salvation also comes the power to overcome sin.

power to overcome sin while living on this earth. Through our faith demonstrated by confident dependence on God's power, we are delivered from evil. Matthew Henry also wrote about this: "Lord, deliver us from the evil of the world, the corruption that is in the world through lust; from the evil of every condition in the world; from the evil of death; from the *sting of death, which is sin;* deliver us from ourselves, from our own evil hearts; deliver us from evil men, that they may not be a snare to us, nor we a prey to them."

We must pray for God's protection from the evil of this world. We must trust God to guide our path and for that path to detour us around the lures, lusts, and other temptations of this world. We must trust God to deliver us from evil every step of the way.

The early believers learned that their best strategy for combat with the evil one was to pray. After listing each part of our spiritual armor, Paul explained the strategy:

> *"Finally, be strong in the Lord and in his mighty power. Put on the full armor of God so that you can take your stand against the devil's schemes. For our struggle is not against flesh and blood, but against rulers, against the authorities, against the powers of this dark world and against the spiritual forces of evil in the heavenly realms. Therefore put on the full armor of God, so that when the day of evil comes, you may be able to stand your ground, and after you have done everything, to stand. Stand firm then, with the belt of truth buckled around your waist, with the breastplate of righteousness in place, and with your feet fitted with the readiness that comes from the gospel of peace. In addition to all this, take up the shield of faith, with which you can extinguish all the flaming arrows of the evil one. Take the helmet of salvation and the sword of the Spirit, which is the word of God.* And pray in the Spirit on all occasions with all kinds of prayers and requests. With this in mind, be alert and always keep on praying for all the saints."*
> (Ephesians 6:10-18, emphasis added)

Jesus taught us to pray this prayer so that we will not be overcome by evil. One writer said this:

> Though God helps us in times of temptation, and though trials can strengthen faith, we should never ask God to give us trials or lead us into temptation. Some Christians want to be heroes for God because they want to prove to him how strong they really are. [They] pray, "Lord, send me a trial so that I can endure it and become even stronger for you." As heroic as that sounds, I've discovered that it's just a form of pride—and stupidity. When you've been through a few ups and downs of the spiritual life, one thing becomes perfectly clear: we are terrible judges of how strong we are, and we have no business telling God when to put trials in our lives. Those matters are best left in His hands. The wise prayer is always, "lead us not into temptation . . .[7]

. . . but deliver us from evil.

Oh God, Please . . .

1. What tempts you most? How do you deal with those temptations?

2. Are there certain times when your guard is down? When? What can you do to prepare for those times?

3. How were Jesus' disciples tempted? What "ways of escape" might they have taken? (To think of these things is purely for fun, and it's OK to use your imagination.)

Pray: *Lord, give me discernment so that I can quickly discover the escape route for every temptation that comes my way. Amen*

CHAPTER 26

For Thine Is the Kingdom, and the Power, and the Glory, For Ever. Amen

"Our Father which art in heaven, hallowed be thy name. Thy kingdom come. Thy will be done in earth, as it is in heaven. Give us this day our daily bread. And forgive us our debts, as we forgive our debtors. And lead us not into temptation, but deliver us from evil: For thine is the kingdom, and the power, and the glory, for ever. Amen."

— MATTHEW 6:9–13 KJV

This chapter's title is the ending of the Lord's Prayer. Most Bible scholars agree that the sentence was not a part of the original manuscripts, that it was added later. It is called a "doxology." Although it might have been added, it is a great way to conclude the prayer. This model prayer takes the pray-er through a conversation that begins and ends at the great throne of God.

I have found great power in learning to pray for an hour using a simple tool that divides the time into five-minute segments. The Lord's Prayer could easily be divided in such a way. Consider the following:

Our Father which art in heaven,

- ⇝ Spend five minutes reflecting on God as your Father who resides in heaven. Tell Him what you see and how you feel about His love for you.

Hallowed be thy name.

- ⇝ Spend five minutes speaking aloud the various names of God. Thank Him for proving names to you at specific times this past week.
- ⇝ Spend five minutes searching Scripture for the names of God, and pray those verses back to Him.

Thy kingdom come. Thy will be done in earth, as it is in heaven.

- ⇝ Spend five minutes focusing on ways Jesus described His Father's kingdom.
- ⇝ Spend five minutes bringing your own will to bow low beneath God's.
- ⇝ Spend five minutes inviting the Holy Spirit to reveal to you God's will for today. Jot your impressions down in a prayer journal.

Give us this day our daily bread.

- ⇝ Spend five minutes thanking God for the ways He meets your physical needs.
- ⇝ Spend five minutes thanking Him for your excess.
- ⇝ Spend five minutes asking Him how He'd like for you to honor Him and impact His kingdom with the resources He's entrusted to you.

And forgive us our debts, as we forgive our debtors.

→ Spend five minutes confessing your sins as the Holy Spirit brings them to mind. Be sure to confess the attitudes that drive your behavior. Consider who you need to forgive and forgive them!

And lead us not into temptation, but deliver us from evil:

→ Spend five minutes declaring your utter dependence on God's leadership and deliverance in specific relationships and situations.

For thine is the kingdom, and the power, and the glory, for ever. Amen.

→ Spend five minutes picturing God on His throne, high and lifted up, capable of responding on behalf of this prayer and exercising His dominion in and through your life.

I love the word *Amen*, which has been translated "so be it." Throughout the Old Testament, worshippers said "Amen" to mean "we agree that which is said is reliable, faithful, and true." In the New Testament "Amen" was said to emphasize truth and surety. Today many worshippers say "Amen" out of habit without much thought to its significance. But when you close your prayer with a hearty "Amen," you are literally saying, "God is faithful to respond to this prayer according to the strength of His might and the truth of His character. So be His response." When you close your prayer with "Amen," you are saying, "Lord, I trust You completely."

Next time you say "Amen," remember what Paul said: "For no matter how many promises God has made, they are 'Yes' in Christ. And so through him the 'Amen' is spoken by us to the glory of God" (2 Corinthians 1:20).

When you pray the Lord's Prayer and when you allow it to direct your infinite variations of this model, always know that the God to whom you speak reigns eternally in the kingdom you were created to inhabit. He reigns in power, and His glory is over all forever and ever. Amen.

Oh God, Please . . .

Go through this chapter again and spend an hour in prayer with your study group or a friend.

The Golden Key of Heaven

"Ask, and it shall be given you; seek, and ye shall find; knock, and it shall be opened unto you: For every one that asketh receiveth; and he that seeketh findeth; and to him that knocketh it shall be opened."

— MATTHEW 7:7–8 KJV

Bishop Winnington Ingram wrote of the secret power of prayer:

> When Queen Victoria was opening the Town Hall of Sheffield, she had put in her hand a little golden key, and she was told as she sat in her carriage that she only had to turn the golden key and in a moment the Town Hall gates of Sheffield would fly open. In obedience to the authority of experts who gave her the directions, she turned the golden key, and in a moment, by the action of electric wires, the Town Hall gates of Sheffield flew open. Exactly in the same way Jesus Christ must know one thing, if he knows anything, and that is, what opens heaven's gates. He must know that; and in his teaching he reiterated over and over again, as if he thought that this was one of the things we should find it hardest to believe; "Ask, and it shall be given; seek, and ye shall find; knock, and it shall be opened unto

you." And I say that if we are justified in believing in the divinity of Christ, then we are justified in going a step further and saying that His authority is good enough to make us believe that the golden key of prayer, if we use it, will open the gates of heaven.[8]

Watchman Nee teaches that because God gave us humans free will He insists on waiting for us to agree with Him freely before He will exert His will on earth. Think about that. If God is all powerful and God's power is all good, if God is all knowing and all God's knowledge is perfect, if God is all loving and His love is unfailing . . . what a tragedy that we don't line our own sin-stained, limited, and weak hearts and minds up with God's! Our prayerlessness leaves most of what God has a mind to do—and most of what God has a will to do—*undone!*

What might happen in your life; what might happen in the lives of your family members; what might happen in your church; what might happen in your neighborhood, your children's schools, your community, and your world . . . if you began to pray?

Pray and find out.

Appendix

How to Spend an Hour in Prayer

An hour in prayer can be spent in many ways. Using this plan as a guide, you will pray through the Lord's Prayer in five-minute increments. Remember to let the Holy Spirit direct your prayer time.

Our Father which are in heaven,

➤ Spend five minutes reflecting on God as your Father who resides in heaven. Tell Him what you see and how you feel about His love for you. Read Revelation 4:2–11 to capture a glimpse of His throne room.

Hallowed be thy name.

➤ Spend five minutes speaking aloud the various names of God. Thank Him for proving names to you at specific times this past week. (See "Names of God" in this appendix.)
➤ Spend five minutes searching Scripture for the names of God, and pray those verses back to Him.

Thy kingdom come. Thy will be done in earth, as it is in heaven.

➤ Spend five minutes focusing on ways Jesus described His Father's kingdom.
➤ Spend five minutes bringing your will to bow low beneath God's.
➤ Spend five minutes inviting the Holy Spirit to reveal to you God's will for today. Jot your impressions down in a prayer journal.

Give us this day our daily bread.

- ➤ Spend five minutes thanking God for the ways He meets your physical needs.
- ➤ Spend five minutes thanking Him for your excess.
- ➤ Spend five minutes asking Him how He'd like for you to honor Him and impact His kingdom with the resources He's entrusted to you.

And forgive us our debts, as we forgive our debtors.

- ➤ Spend five minutes confessing your sins as the Holy Spirit brings them to mind. Be sure to confess the attitudes that drive your behavior. Consider who you need to forgive and forgive them.

And lead us not into temptation, but deliver us from evil:

- ➤ Spend five minutes declaring your utter dependence on God's leadership and deliverance in specific relationships and situations.

For thine is the kingdom, and the power, and the glory, for ever. Amen.

- ➤ Spend five minutes picturing God on His throne, high and lifted up, capable of responding on behalf of this prayer and exercising His dominion in and through your life.

Praying the Names of God

The character of God is revealed in His name. A great way to pray is to call on the "name of the Lord." In fact, God's Word tells us not once, not twice, but three times that "everyone who calls on the name of the Lord will be saved" (Joel 2:32; Acts 2:21; Romans 10:13).

I've told you once, I've told you twice—three times I've told you—"Everyone who calls on the name of the Lord will be saved!"

⤞ Are you alone? Call on *Jehovah Shammah*, "God is present with me" (see Ezekiel 48:35).
⤞ Are you lost and afraid? Call on *Jehovah Rohi*, "God is my shepherd" (see Psalm 23:1).
⤞ Are you in need? Call on *Jehovah Jireh*, "The Lord my provider" (see Genesis 22:14).
⤞ Are you sick? Call on *Jehovah Rophe*, "The Lord who healeth me" (see Exodus 15:26).
⤞ Are you guilty? Call on *Jehovah Tsidkenu*, "God is my righteousness" (see Jeremiah 23:6).
⤞ Have you messed up? Call on *Jehovah M'Kiddish*, "God is my sanctification" (see Leviticus 20:8).
⤞ Are you stressed or distressed because of your circumstances? Call on *Jehovah Shalom*, "God is my peace" (see Judges 6:24).
⤞ Are you overwhelmed by conflict and confrontation? Call on *Jehovah Nissi*, "God is my banner" (see Exodus 17:15).

Praise God for who He is and for what He does.

Scriptural Basis for Praying in Jesus' Name

➣ John 14:13—"Whatever you ask in My name, I will do it so that the Father may be glorified in the Son" (HCSB).

➣ John 14:14—"If you ask Me anything in My name, I will do it" (HCSB).

➣ John 15:16—"You did not choose Me, but I chose you. I appointed you that you should go out and produce fruit and that your fruit should remain, so that whatever you ask the Father in My name, He will give you" (HCSB).

➣ John 16:23—"In that day you will not ask Me anything. 'I assure you: Anything you ask the Father in My name, He will give you'" (HCSB).

➣ John 16:24—"Until now you have asked nothing in My name. Ask and you will receive, that your joy may be complete" (HCSB).

➣ John 16:26–27—"In that day you will ask in My name. I am not telling you that I will make requests to the Father on your behalf. For the Father Himself loves you, because you have loved Me and have believed that I came from God" (HCSB).

Creating a Prayer Place

Designate a specific time to pray—not so much a time on the clock as a time in your schedule. For instance, you don't have to pray at 6:00 a.m. every day, but you might determine to pray just after you get out of bed and pour that first cup of coffee.

Designate a place to pray. This can be a favorite chair, your porch swing, even a spot in your closet (that's where my husband prays; he took Jesus' instruction literally!).

Take specific tools with you to your place of prayer. Those tools might consist of a journal, your Bible, a hymnal, or worship music on your iPod. When I went on a mission trip with a friend, we were often sleeping together in small quarters. Still, every morning she had her quiet time, and she established her quiet place by putting in earphones and listening to praise music on her iPod.

Keep your tools in your prayer place. You might use a basket or a spot on a table or the chair itself. Just make sure you have everything you need in your prayer place. Otherwise the enemy will use the distraction to gobble up your prayer time. I can't tell you how many times I've gotten up from my prayer place to find a pen, then decided to load the dishes quickly, then looked through yesterday's paper, emptied the trash, gone to the bathroom, and suddenly realized that I missed my prayer time.

Don't let that happen to you. Make your time for prayer a priority. Select a quiet place, and stock it with your prayer tools.

Quiet Time Recipe

Warm your heart by singing a favorite hymn or chorus.

Ingredients:

Bible
devotional magazine or book
notebook
pen
index cards

1. First, ask God to speak to your heart during this time. Tell Him you will obey Him today.
2. Read your Bible (either a chapter or the passage recommended in your devotional magazine or book).
3. Write down key words, phrases, or verses in your notebook.
4. Write down what you think God is saying to you about what you've read today.
5. Pray. (You can write your prayers or pray out loud.)
6. List special prayer concerns in your notebook. (Come back later and place a date beside the concerns when God answers your prayers.)
7. Use the index card to record verses you'd like to memorize. Try to memorize one Bible verse each week.
8. Thank God for meeting you today. Keep listening as He talks to you throughout your day.

Dealing with Trash Baskets

*"Forgive us our trash baskets as we forgive those
who put trash in our baskets."*

Unforgiveness is a barrier to prayer. When you harbor resentment, offense, or bitterness toward someone else and then pray, your prayer is no more effective than is your conversation when your cell phone is dead. How sad! How many people spend their energy pouring their hearts out to God while harboring unforgiveness in their spirits? How long do they wait for God to answer their prayers?

If you want to release a torrential downpour of God's power in your life, then invite the Holy Spirit to rid your heart of unforgiveness:

Lord, show me who has offended me. (In the space provided, jot the names of the people who come to your mind)

_____

_____

_____

_____

_____

_____

_____

_____

_____

Now declare some choices:
Father, I choose to forgive: (List their names here along with a brief description of what they did.)

_____

_____

_____

_____

_____

_____

_____

_____

_____

_____

_____

_____

_____

I choose to let go of my "right" to hold on to my anger.
I choose to let go of my "right" to harbor bitterness.
I choose to tame my tongue and make it a slave to my will.
I choose to line my will up with Yours.
Thank You for forgiving me.
Amen

Endnotes

[1] Selwyn Hughes, *Prayer, the Greatest Power: Everyday Light for Your Journey* (Nashville, TN: Crusade for World Revival, 2001), 28, 32, 34–35.

[2] Watchman Nee, *Let Us Pray* (New York: Christian Literature Crusade, 1995), 18–20.

[3] Ben Patterson, *Prayer Devotional Bible* (Grand Rapids, MI: Zondervan, 2004), 384.

[4] Jennifer Kennedy Dean, *Heart's Cry, Principles of Prayer* (Birmingham, AL: New Hope Publishers 1992), 10.

[5] Ben Patterson, *Prayer Devotional Bible* (Grand Rapids, MI: Zondervan, 2004), 1146.

[6] J. Gilchrist Lawson, *George Muller* (Christian Biography Resources, www.wholesomewords.com).

[7] Mark Galli and James S. Bell Jr., *The Complete Idiot's Guide to Prayer* (New York: Penguin Group, 2004), 67.

[8] Herbert Lockyear, *All the Prayers of the Bible* (Grand Rapids, MI: Zondervan, 1959), 193.

My Notes from This Study

My Notes from This Study

My Notes from This Study

My Notes from This Study

My Notes from This Study

Leighann McCoy

is the prayer and women's minister at Thompson Station Church in Thompson Station, TN, where her husband Tom is the senior pastor.

Her books include *Spiritual Warfare for Women, Women Overcoming Fear,* and *Meet Me at the Manger and I'll Lead You to the Cross.* Leighann lives in Franklin, TN, and is the mother of two daughters, one son, and a son-in-law: Mikel (Austin), Kaleigh, and T.J. Her favorite role is that of Nana to her granddaughter, Misty.